SHAMAN'S DRUM

Shamanic Healing with real accounts of
Journeys of Healing and Soul Retrieval

Caroline Dawley

Pathway of Peace

PALM HARBOR, FLORIDA

Copyright © 2018 by Caroline Dawley

All rights reserved. No part of this publication may be reproduced, distributed or transmitted in any form or by any means, without prior written permission.

Caroline Dawley/Pathway of Peace
1219 Florida Ave
Palm Harbor, Florida 34684
www.shamanismthenewbeginning.blogspot.com

Publisher's Note: This is a work of non-fiction. Only client's names have been changed. Book Layout © 2017 BookDesignTemplates.com

Book Layout © 2017 BookDesignTemplates.com

Shaman's Drum/ Caroline Dawley. -- 1st ed.
ISBN 13: 978-1985663329

DEDICATION

I dedicate this book to my children and grandchildren seven generations into the future.

And to all my clients and friends, my fellow Dreamers who are awakening the Dream, are working for the Light, who have Vision and Intention for the Highest Good for The Whole, assisting in the Healing and Ascension of the Earth into the New Program of Earth as a Star.

Other Books by Caroline Dawley:

Pathway of Peace: Journey to the New Earth

*"As we heal ourselves we heal our family.
As we heal our family we heal the community.
As we heal the community we heal the Nation.
As we heal the nation we heal the world".*

Algonquin Medicine Song:

*"HeYa HeYa HeYa Ho, HeYa HeYa Ho,
HeYa HeYa HeYa Ho, HeYa HeYa Ho.
HeYa HeYa HeYa Ho, HeYa HeYa Ho,
HeYa HeYa HeYa Ho, HeYa HeYa Ho
MeGwich MeGwich MeGwich MeGwich,
MeGuich MeGuich MeGuich."*.

——QUOTATION SOURCE
ALGONQUIN PRAYER AND STATEMENT TO THE UNITED
NATIONS GENERAL ASSEMBLY FOR THE HEALING OF
MAN AND THE EARTH. 1993, U.N. FIRST PEOPLES
PROPHECIES, "CRY OF THE EARTH" SUMMIT AS SPOKEN
BY WILLIAM COMMANDA.

A SPECIAL NOTE TO THE READER

This book is an inspired work to illuminate the Ancient Practice of Shamanism to bring clarity and understanding of its Power to heal in our contemporary world. During Soul Retrieval, you Journey to the sound of the Drum to view your Shadow self and integrate with your Soul Light in the Heart of the world where you find your life purpose. Worlds open as you leave ordinary reality and journey to spiritual realms, embracing the Light; discovering your gifts, power animals, and destiny.

During Shamanic Healing, the Shaman seeks to clear your emotional body, mental body, and in your physical body; as you integrate all three, you become one with your Soul. Soul Retrieval is the Journey to retrieve fragments of your lost Soul caused by Trauma. Traumatic events from the past live in the body as blocked energy, unaddressed emotional trauma lives in our cells as cell memory and predispose our bodies to illness or dis-ease.

During the Soul Retrieval, the trauma and resulting dis-ease caused from it are healed. Shaman's have Vision and can see beyond ordinary life, Creating Sacred Space, they guide you on a Journey into the Heart; illuminating the Shadow with healing Light, you are changed by the experience as you receive healing, your spiritual gifts, and integrate with your Soul. You are set free to begin the Hero's Journey to your Destiny.

Healing happens when trauma is identified, the shadow illuminated; opening windows of consciousness that allow you to Journey beyond the illusion of separation and the veils that have kept you in isolation. When the first three circles of relationship are sound, you are then able to connect to Spirit in all life forms. Worlds of consciousness are opened as you journey to your destiny as eternal souls.

The Soul Retrieval Journey connects you with your higher mind, with the Light, where you raise awareness and release patterns that keep you bound in lower vibrational patterns of dysfunction and illness. You create your reality with your thoughts. Shamanic healing offers mental, emotional, and body clearing through illuminating your mind with Truth, freeing you from limiting points of view and expanding awareness of the Whole. Shamans help you raise the frequency of the inner Light, becoming One with your Soul, you integrate Mind, Body, and Spirit. You now realize your Divine Self.

The Shaman first creates sacred space where the healing is to take place by cleansing it with smoke from the herbs, drawing a circle of protection, and calling in the sacred powers of the four directions, asking for guidance during the healing. This transforms the space into a circle containing the wholeness of the Universe and all of the Medicine helpers in the visible and invisible worlds. The Drum, Rattle, Vision quest, and Medicine song help the Shaman enter spiritual realms and make direct contact with the powers that will reveal the cure. The Shaman restores balance by listening to the inner instructions and depends on Vision to see beyond the illness or imbalance, beyond ordinary reality. Working with the Medicine Wheel and years of personal Spiritual Visions builds relationships and communication with Spirit animals, Guides, inner Wisdom. It is these experiences that form the inner-connectedness of life from which we draw most of our Medicine Power. Shamanism is based on experience, a calling received through Vision and Initiation that requires commitment, willingness to answer the call, and a passion to help heal suffering humanity.

Caroline Dawley

CONTENTS

1. Shamanic Healing 9
2. Shaman's Death 15
3. Susan's Story 17
4. The Seven Layers of Separation 19
5. Soul Journeying – The Vision Quest 23
6. Awaken the Healer Within 31
7. Holly's Story 37
8. Shamanism 39
9. Maria's Story 45
10. Soul Retrieval – What is It? 47
11. Shamanic Healing with Sound 53
12. Create Sacred Space 57
13. Mary's Story 61
14. Animal Totems and Their Significance 63
15. Journey to Retrieve Your Spirit Animals 69
16. Cassie's Story 71
17. Finding the Original Wound 75
18. Journey to the Womb of Mother Earth 79
19. Adam's Story 83
20. Soul Loss 85
21. Soul Contracts 87
22. Angela's Story 91
23. Hero's Journey in Search of Your Sacred Destiny 93
24. Chamber of Grace 95

25. Illuminating Your Shadow 97
26. Becoming Whole 101
27. See with the Eyes of Your Heart 105
28. Life is a Ceremony 109
29. The Story of Jumping Mouse 115
30. Message of the Light... 125

1. Shamanic Healing

We are Servants of the Earth. The first meeting of the Shamans took place in Austria in 1982. Shamans, healers, medicine man, and scientists sat in a circle and concentrated on the single theme; the healing of the Earth and the healing of man. There was agreement that our disconnection from our natural environment has put the Earth out of balance to such a degree that we'll have to do everything in our power to bring it back into balance if life is to be guaranteed at all. The outcome of the meeting is this quote:

"Man must find his place within the whole once more. He can only proceed by reuniting himself with his divine origins, now, while he is still on Earth, still has a body. Man has forgotten that the Divine Spirit within him is a source of power and wisdom. This is his Higher Self, his inner healer. We came here to help those who desire to advance to the source of their power. Medicine exposes the barriers that stop man (woman) from reaching his/her own Center, where he knows his mission intuitively, with the clarity of animal instinct. In his/her higher self, "man" is one with God and one with the infinite spirit. It is the higher self that receives the ideas of the All One, All-Knowing, and Eternal Cosmic Spirit. Man can only know of his duty, his vision, his dream, his/ her medicine through this connection that links her with the Divine. Only through continuous dialogue with a higher authority

can one become a Medicine Man or Medicine Woman; in everything they do Medicine will be reflected, Medicine for healing their fellow man, healing of the earth, and healing of the whole."

        Laurence Temple, The Shining Brother

MESSAGE OF THE SHAMANS

"The time has come when the mysteries of the age shall be revealed to all who desire light upon their path that they may approach the Center of all Power and Life. For a new spirit is within the world and wo/man throws off the lead strings and will no longer follow blindly the blind leaders. She will accept instruction only from those who can perceive the Invisible and hear the unspoken word, who are filled with the Spirit and who speak with Inner Knowledge and have escaped from the bondage of creeds and the inherited beliefs of past generations. For the Soul of wo/man requires freedom for the growth of the New Age and strength to carry the burden of greater responsibilities. Therefore, upon many will be poured forth the Gifts of Spirit that Light may penetrate the Darkness, and humanity be reborn nearer to the Divine image.

  This is the Day of Days when many Forces meet, and much is shattered in the impact, yet in the Infinite Mind is the Supreme Thought, the Creative urge towards perfection and we who are at ONE with these vast waves of Power, and all our being is given to this invincible direction of the thought forms of God. For His children work each in their Degree and the Power is transformed by the creative activity of His Ministers. There is no break in the chain between the least and the greatest. The Creative Power flows through all and each is a partaker in the Divine Plan and gives that which she/he has to the Universe."

(Lawrence Temple, the Shining Brother, (1970) London: Psychic Press, 1941 pg. 185-186)

Healing is a pathway that begins within ourselves. Learning our own patterns of imbalance and healing ourselves is the path of the Shaman. Shamanism is an ancient spiritual practice of the Indigenous Medicine People. More people are experiencing healing, transformation and awakening during Soul Retrieval Journeying; a healing practice that heals you after journeying to discover your original wound. Journeying to the sound of the Drum takes you beyond the veils of illusion where you travel to retrieve you lost soul part. Soul Retrieval heals your past, reclaiming your divine blueprint.

Discovering ancient shamanic practices while journeying into the Dream World, you awaken your Dream and manifest the divine blueprint of your oversoul. Connecting with your spirit guide, with your higher-self, you learn once again to walk in the wisdom of innocence and joy. You open the eyes of your Heart and once again live life fully, seeing life and all its beauty, you will reclaim your highest reality.

Shamanism reconnects you to our roots found in nature and connects us with our higher consciousness. You will become one with nature and committed to the Oneness of humanity and creation. Healing and restoring within yourself and others is the Shamanic Pathway of Spiritual Awakening. The Path of Shamanism expands our awareness and provides inner journeys where we access hidden worlds and dimensions with sources of wisdom and power for healing ourselves and the planet. We will rediscover ourselves, our indigenous Heart, reconnecting with our spirit guides, spirit teachers, our ancestors and power animals. As we enter the field of the visionary and see nature through the eyes of our heart, we explore our illness, trauma, and healing through the Wisdom of Indigenous Spiritual Medicine.

In Shamanism, the Shaman guides you as you experience your original wound and heal the past trauma. Almost everyone has emotional and physical wounds caused by trauma during their lifetime. Soul retrieval returns the part of the soul that splits apart. During a Soul Retrieval session, clients have remarked, "I regained my innocence!". Another, "I needed this in my life." "I'm given the gift of Peace." And, "I'm completely changed!"

When we experience traumatic events, it is possible for a portion of the soul to separate, taking with it a part of our essential self. This soul loss can manifest in many ways; including illness, emotional blockage, fear, and insecurity. Fortunately, it is possible to enter non-linear time, the timeless now, to recover the lost soul part, heal events that happened in the past, and reclaim our destiny.

I mentored with Chief Leon Shenandoah of the Iroquois people, Grandmother Two Worlds, Twylia Nitch's Wisdom Wheel teachings, and in energy healing practices; receiving my certificate as a Reiki Master in 1999. I am guided by my spiritual high being; or spirit guide who journeys with me during a Shamanic healing session. Training with the Iroquois has taught me that there are 7 veils associated directly with our energy centers. These veils cause us to only see from the limited view of the ego mind and are called our shadow. After a shamanic healing, the veils are removed, and we can view from a spiritual perspective. This is because the soul retrieval journey involves renegotiating soul contracts and embracing an expansive world view as we journey to spiritual realms. Much of the soul journey is viewed as archetypes and symbolic meanings. It is the task of the Shaman to interpret the story being told and the illumination that occurs when the Soul is retrieved, and destiny glimpsed. Shamanic journeying is rich in image and is a journey of the awakening Soul.

My own journey into shamanism was guided by my desire to become whole. By healing my emotional wounds, I learned to have unconditional love for myself and others, and a desire to help those who are suffering. Soul Retrieval accomplishes healing in a few sessions compared to mainstream therapy that could take years; yet as bridges are built combining therapy and Shamanism, valuable healing results. While walking the Good Red Road and the path of the wounded healer, I learned to transform the grief, pain, anger, and shame that lived within me into sources of strength and compassion.

Healing begins within as you learn the patterns of imbalance in your system. A Shaman assists her client as he/she enters alternate spirit dimensions and becomes empowered during the healing process. The Shaman guides you on the journey on a spiritual plane empowering you to begin healing yourself. Shamanism is built on the foundation that change is an inevitable part of life, and only you have the power to make the changes necessary to manifest the reality you seek. Our spiritual self is the part of us that guides us through life by providing us with intuitive guidance and directing us to succeed in life and learn from its many lessons. When the spiritual side is weak, we can no longer hear it speaking to us, and can feel as if we've lost our way.

2. Shaman's Death

"When we reconstruct the fragments of our Dreams, we bring an aliveness to the spirit that allows the imagination to go beyond the need to survive. Imagining a better world allows us to actively participate in creating our dreams...."

Jamie Sams, Thirteen Original Clan Mothers

In the beginning of our spiritual awakening, we come to the end of ourselves and can't go on as we are; that's what I call the Shaman's death. We cannot move forward in life to discover life's meaning; until we come to a place of complete surrender of our shadow self, and a willingness to release our ego self. The Shaman's death is not easy, but a true initiation signifying the beginning of our spiritual journey to wholeness, freedom, and finding our sacred destiny. As we journey into the Light, healing our past trauma and illuminating our shadow, we become our own best healer. Then, we may begin to help heal the world.

My own journey led to a vision of a cliff, a jumping off point where I was faced with my own death. Letting go, taking the leap, quite certain I would die; yet there was another voice calling me, assuring me. In that moment, I felt wings gently lifting me as peace filled my being, a peace I had not known. You must die before you can rise, you must bend low to find the inner journey through the heart, into the spiritual realms. Sacrificing everything you know in the exterior world of illusion, you journey to find the Light within.

I was very ill and broken when I was 25 years old. Migraines, ulcers, sciatica, with unbearable pain, daily. I had no hope. I had been to many allopathic Drs. who treated the symptoms but were unable to heal the root of my pain. At that time a new awareness of life was growing in my innermost being. I began searching for the cause of dis-ease, and dis-harmony, vs. life, health, and wellbeing. I began to understand the law of cause and effect; and the importance of having a right relationship with God, with myself, with Mother Earth and with others. I understood that dis-ease and disharmony in relationships is caused by a breakdown in our relationship with our Source, our Creator. The effect of this causes broken relationships with family and friends and is manifested as disharmony and dis-ease. By surrendering my brokenness, I released my true self to begin the journey to healing and finding my Sacred Destiny.

My intention as Shaman and Healer, is to awaken the Consciousness of Oneness, thereby healing the Planet and understanding that we are all interconnected in the great circle of life, also referred to as the Medicine Wheel, or Sacred Hoop. It's our responsibility to nurture, cultivate, and create the future we desire for our Children and Grandchildren seven generations into the future; first by healing yourself, then the whole collective. Healing your ancestral lineage resonates backward seven generations and forward seven generations as you heal your original wound and reclaim your sacred destiny. I use the analogy of the Seed. The Seed contains the whole blueprint. By grounding your vision and planting the Seed of your highest vision, you cultivate love, and regeneration for the Earth, manifesting a bright New Dawn. Life is a circle of planting, tending, harvesting, and reaping the rewards of your service to the whole; planting seeds that produce abundance for future generations, to the seventh generation.

3. Susan's Story

Susan was a new client who come into my office explaining that after being on a trip, she was stressed and exhausted. She asked if I could do a healing session with her. We agreed that cleansing and clearing her aura and aligning her chakras would be a good beginning. Using Shamanic healing and Reiki energy healing, I first cleansed, cleared and opened her chakras. Then using the rattle, I loosened and pulled off energetic layers of pain and trauma. I put her in an energy cocoon and continued to smudge with sage and rattle, and while working with Susan and my guides, cut energetic cords that had been draining her energy for years.

I was instructed by my higher self to lead Susan to a new beginning in her life. We began with a guided meditation into her Sacred Garden where we walked a pathway to a bridge. Asking for a significant life to be shown, Susan crossed the bridge and saw a man whom she had known for years, waiting for her. While talking with him, she realized she needed to bring closure to their relationship that had become a great strain, explaining that they lived countries apart. They said, "good bye." Returning to her Sacred Garden, Susan reflected on that past life, and realized she was ready to move forward on her life journey.

Again, in meditation, we began in her Sacred Garden, walking a pathway to a bridge; symbolically spanning past, present, and future.

Susan crossed the bridge, once again, but this time the man was not waiting for her. As she kept walking on her path, she felt free and excited about her future. Up ahead and on the distance, she saw a man waiting for her. However, she wasn't ready yet to proceed, that would be in the future. I smudged Susan's aura and continued to unify and purify her Chakras with the singing bowl, clearing her electromagnetic field for optimum vibration. She said, "I feel like a new person". I then ended our session disconnecting from the energies, giving thanks to all the invisible helpers who made this healing possible.

4. The Seven Layers of Separation

"On all seven paths of transformation, every fragment of truth that is retrieved and every piece of awareness that is remembered, reshapes our perception of our human identity. The seven sacred paths are our journey home to our authentic spiritual identities and our divine connection to the Great Mystery".

Jamie Sams, Dancing the Dream

Awakening refers to the retrieval of the fragmented soul consciousness. Retrieving the lost soul fragments creates wholeness and an awakened spirit that is fully inside the physical body. As we heal and retrieve forgotten parts of our human potential, we can then develop our gifts and become fully conscious and aware of the Oneness and interconnection of all that is. The awakening occurs when we decide to become whole and is a process of spiritual growth that begins the healing journey in search of wellbeing and our full human potential. When we heal our past wounds and dysfunctional behaviors, we begin to move beyond the veils of limiting beliefs held in our consciousness that prevented us from being whole spiritual human beings. We begin to discover our lost gifts and our divine purpose for living. The layers of separation prevent us from remembering our connection to Creator.

Our Aura is made up of energetic threads that are connected to all our experiences; it is formed in layers around our body. Every experience we have had since birth and in past lives creates an energetic egg-shaped aura connected to each chakra that runs along our spine from the top of our head to the bottom of our feet. Each of the chakras, or energy pathways has its own qualities. The Mayans refer to this as being like an onion, our challenge is to peel away the layers of the illusion that keep us in the consciousness of separation.

The first layer keeps us from remembering the oneness of the universe and that everything is interconnected. The second layer is created by forgetting our real identity and Spiritual Essences and that we are one with spirit and Creator. The third layer of separation is created through the limiting awareness that there is more than what we see, feel, and hear with our physical senses. We are programmed according to the teachings of our environment; our parents, teachers, and educational programs. The fourth layer is created when we develop our emotions; many of us are taught to control, repress, and even deny our feelings. When we are unable to express our true feelings and emotions, we don't know who we are, and may feel lost or abandoned. Only when this layer of separation is lifted can we gain access to the divine will of Creator that exists as part of our Spiritual Essence allowing us to freely express our heart-felt feelings and to be our authentic self.

The fifth layer is composed of our belief systems; our decisions, limited beliefs, and assumptions about everything we experience in life. When we begin to heal, or we retrieve our lost soul part, we experience a surge of life force energy. This energy gives us flashes of intuitive inner awareness. It is then that we continue to grow spiritually and begin to have universal consciousness. This is when we begin to use our gifts we were born with and begin our soul's journey to reach our Destiny.

The sixth layer of separation is created when we shut down our perceptions of anything that is not solid, we have no awareness of spirit; we perceive life only as physical. This layer blocks access to spiritual growth and awareness. The seventh layer is caused by our personal sense and the ego concepts of who we are. As we remove the layers, we gain awareness of a spiritual state of "Grace" where we see our divine connections. Our human spirit takes its place as One with the Creator and can reach its human destiny as an eternal soul, experiencing "heaven on earth."

There are many relationships that we experience to shape our spiritual essence in both the visible and invisible worlds. To expand our relationships to include all part of creation, we must first have a sound relationship with our Creator by communicating gratitude and opening our heart to the Great Mystery. The second relationship is to our self and is maintained by honoring our mind, body, and spirit. This includes detaching from negative energy and anything that limits our growth, that is not honoring our highest good. The third relationship that we must maintain is our relationship to others; that is maintained through personal integrity and being loving and respectful to all our relations in the circle of life.

During a Soul Retrieval Journey, the Shaman interprets the dream and symbols discovered on the pathway to healing. In this way, the healing begins when trauma is identified; the shadow illuminated; opening windows of consciousness that allow us to journey beyond the illusion of separation and the layers that have kept us in isolation. We learn that we are not alone. The Shaman recreates the message after the soul retrieval journey, retrieving the fragments of soul lost. When the first three circles of relationship are sound, we are then able to connect to spirit in all life forms. Worlds of consciousness are opened as we journey to our destiny as eternal souls.

5. Soul Journeying – The Vision Quest

"We are created by Creator to be people of vision. To be able to soar beyond ordinary life."

Frank Fools Crow, Lakota

My prayer today; Creator, shine your Light on my path so that I can see; may I have eyes like Eagle, strength like Bear, dedication and loyalty like Wolf, and a big heart to love everyone. Great Spirit lead me on the path to the New Dawn.

We are created to have spiritual vision to see our sacred destiny. We intend for our higher dream to awaken, some call the awakening of the dream held in the collective consciousness of humanity. At first, we may see only a glimpse of the Light, so far in the distance; or we may hear the call, see the vision that cannot be denied. All of us have incarnated on Earth with a divine purpose, Soul Retrieval retrieves those latent gifts and abilities by illuminating the shadow, shining Light on your sacred destiny.

The Tree of Life stands through time, having roots buried deep into the very core of the Great Mother, branches reaching to the sky where angels live among the clouds. Abandoned by man long ago when his soul was split apart; humanity began it long trek of dysfunction and trauma, separated from the Light of its Source. Without a Soul man/woman wanders in the wasteland like dead men walking. Yet the Tree stands. The call is heard, subtle at first. It may be a sound far off, or a light beckoning in the distance. A glimpse of a shining Mt. with Light shining above its peaks.

The vision quest begins the journey in search of our Soul, the essential self that we cannot live without. It shines on another life, a deeper, fuller life that we know because we know is real. To journey beyond ordinary life, beyond pain and suffering, we must follow spirit's lead into the unknown. We cannot enter without a guide. It is often our Spiritual guide, who leads us on the path.

We begin by holding a vision of the highest and greatest picture we can imagine; the picture will begin to unfold a new reality. The spiritual journey is the greatest adventure you will ever live. We are asked to give, in order to receive; sacrifice old beliefs, addictions that lead to dysfunction, and to know the illusion; that ordinary life is not all there is. In our collective consciousness, we have a Dream; it is awakened by the Bright Light, illuminating all that can be if we commit to the vison and begin our journey, becoming a seeker of Truth. Dedication to the path and years of learning in the higher school of Spiritual Law. It's between you and the Creator and Mother Earth, you are their child; Bright Morning Star, and you were born with a Sacred Destiny.

Visionaries can see what might be possible rather than what is. They see into the future with their strong intuition and can see the possibilities as real. Their talent is often used to bring forth creative endeavors that benefit societies and cultures. They always have the big picture in mind seeing what is just beyond the horizon. The light side of the Visionary is highly creative and optimistic seeing the future as full of hope rather than doom.

Visioning is the practice of awakening the dream and receiving the visions that lead us on our Spiritual Journey to Unity and Wholeness of body, mind, and spirit. The Vision Quest is a growing spiritual discipline extended to the lifelong pursuit of wisdom; of body and soul. Self-reliance is when one depends upon our own visions and dreams to give direction and illuminate our path. Drumming, song, and rattles call in our many allies and Great Spirit to assist us on our healing path. Healing with sound attunes oneself to the vibration of Great Spirit and a belief and partnership with the invisible worlds. When we become one with the "Conscious Collective" or the high mind of Creator, the ability to make personal contact within a sense of nonlinear time occurs when we enter the silence; moving inter-dimensionally, past, present, and future is experienced now. We experience oneness with Spirit that gives knowledge that the Great Spirit is in everything, and can aid us in the stone, the plant, the animal, and human kingdoms. We know that we are One with all of creation. When we embrace and practice reverence for life and an understanding that Mother Earth is our true Mother and is sacred, we become committed to our responsibility as stewards and co-creators of the Earth. Visioning requires a total commitment to one's belief that pervades every aspect of life and enables one to walk in balance with Creator, with oneself, and with our environment.

In Shamanism, the central focus of medicine power is the reliance on our personal Visions as our guiding force. And one must have a total commitment. The seeker of Truth must live the commitment every moment and believe in the love, in the unity, and cooperation of all forms of life, and honor and love All Our Relations.

The Vision Quest is a spiritual experience; a quest for wisdom of body, mind, and soul. It is the search for the "essential self", and to be one with our Soul. Medicine is anything that brings healing and balance in all areas of life, and oneness with the Great Mystery. Visioning is our continued quest for wisdom; this power enables us to obtain personal contact with the world of spirits, and ascend beyond the world of Illusion, which veils the Great Mystery. Seeking truth, we must have an attitude of acceptance for the unknown, this is an expanded worldview. To awaken the dream of Unity Consciousness and wholeness, we must learn to walk on the earth in good balance, in a sacred way. This means we must learn to relate to Mother Earth and each other and all of creation. All relations are sacred, the whole Earth is sacred.

To experience visioning and to awaken the dream, the experience itself is brought about by music, drumming, singing your power song, and smudging with the sacred plant. All aid us to shift our conscious awareness. You may see the appearance of light, illumination, or experience awakening. Your spirit guide may manifest as a light being or as a guide, as an animal, you know that this is real by your feelings of love and peace. You may have an awareness of the Oneness of Creation.

Meditation is a way of entering the silence where you have insights, and you're given messages. You see symbols, and strong Impressions may be received, or you may be given a secret name. Listening helps us awaken our dreams so that we can manifest them in our lives. Decide on the time, the time is now, to be your best and fulfill Your Divine mission. When you connect with your dream; you see it, plan it, and live it. Choose your Highest Potential now, shine your light and be your best.

I use the analogy of the Seed. The Seed contains the whole blueprint. Ground your vision by planting the Seed of your highest vision. Cultivate, love, tend to your seed, and it will manifest a beautiful future. You will receive as your give. Life is a circle of planting, tending, harvesting, and reaping the rewards of our service, tending our Garden to produce abundant seeds for future generations, to the seventh generation.

<u>Meditation Exercise</u>: *Create Sacred Space and begin by listening to the sound of the Drum.*

The Mirror reflects things that we can't always see, like a hologram it contains all parts of the whole. Still water is like a mirror, look into the water and see the whole creation reflected. You are now entering the dream; feel yourself rising up, higher and higher, becoming lighter and lighter. Your awareness is heightened as you look from a higher perspective. Become aware of any guides, totems, or beings of light that have come to assist you. Greet them with love. Now ask these questions; Who am I? What is My Soul Purpose? Allow yourself to enter the dream. See the reflection of your real self as you integrate and become one. Be aware of any symbols, feelings, animals, colors. Now ask the question what is my path? What steps do I take to manifest my dream or to gain the skills I need to accomplish this purpose? Allow a message or symbols to unfold ask questions. Now see yourself fulfilling the plan and becoming your dream. Feel what it feels like to be self-realized. Become one with your Medicine Power. See yourself living it now.

One of my favorite masters is the late Dr. Wayne Dyer. A man who expanded his consciousness to be inclusive of all sacred paths. By stepping beyond fear and limiting boundaries, he allowed his inspiration to lead him on an ever-evolving pathway to enlightenment.

"Inspiration", said Dr. Dyer, "is to have a mind that transcends all limitations."

Enlightenment is to be One with the Shining One, the inner soul rising on a new dawn. To have a glimpse of that Light, even for an instant, begins the heart's calling. There is a higher path, a steeper path that leads through the Heart and the great Tree of Life. Before you rise, you must first bow low and follow the root to the beginning that is found in the Sacred Garden. The way to heaven is the heart's calling to come home. There is a way, Listen.

In the silence, you will hear the call. It may be in the stream rushing, or the whisper of the trees in the wind. It may be a voice calling your name, the name that only you know. It's your path; take the leap, go for the challenge. No other adventure compares to the inner journey of the soul in its long trek home. You will not be disappointed.

Begin with your thoughts to change the world you are experiencing. Decide to be one with Spirit and you will begin to see a whole new world unfold. Change negative thoughts into positive, life affirming thoughts that will attract peace and love. The law states that like attracts like. Keep your mind up in the good mind and be grateful for everything that supports life; see everything through the eyes of the spirit and bless everything you think and see. Make sacred the very ground you walk on, everyplace the sol of your foot touches, may it be for peace and love.

Solitude is the place where you begin to communicate with your soul. Where spirit speaks in messages that only you know; symbols with deep meaning open the windows of consciousness, to let in more light. Devotion, meditation, fasting, contemplation, reflection are all pathways of solitude. By purposely and consciously entering the inner dimension of the soul you build lines of communication. I always believe we have a direct line to God's ear, to pick up the phone and speak from your heart, knowing that you are heard. Your purpose for being here, your personal and unique path is between you and Creator. It is your responsibility to build your faith, that is the bridge from evil to light. Listen to the voice inside called your intuition, it will never mislead you. Believe in the visions that you have, give thanks for them, then see them manifest in your life.

Gratitude sustains the Earth, supports life and beauty, and feeds your spiritual Light. The Essene teachings speak of Gratitude; "To be grateful is to stand in heaven on earth". It is a state of your high heart. When you can be grateful for everything under the Sun, you begin to sustain the Earth, bringing holy life streams into your life. The Light you emit grows brighter as you learn the miracle of creation. By giving thanks, all life continues to evolve in consciousness and the Tree Blossoms.

Forgiveness releases you from bondage to the ego and human suffering opening the gate to an initiation of the Light, bringing peace and releasing bound up emotions, forgiveness opens the dam and lets the pent-up feelings flow. There is a cleansing and transformation as love blossoms with a new understanding that we are One; I forgive you, I forgive myself. We are both set free as healing begins. Offer up to spirit anything in your shadow that indicates a spirit of resentment, envy, or bitterness. Invite the sweet spirit of love into your heart to heal all the wounds for yourself and your family. Begin to heal the branch of the Tree of Life on which your Ancestors dwell, and send healing into the future seven generations, and to those yet unborn.

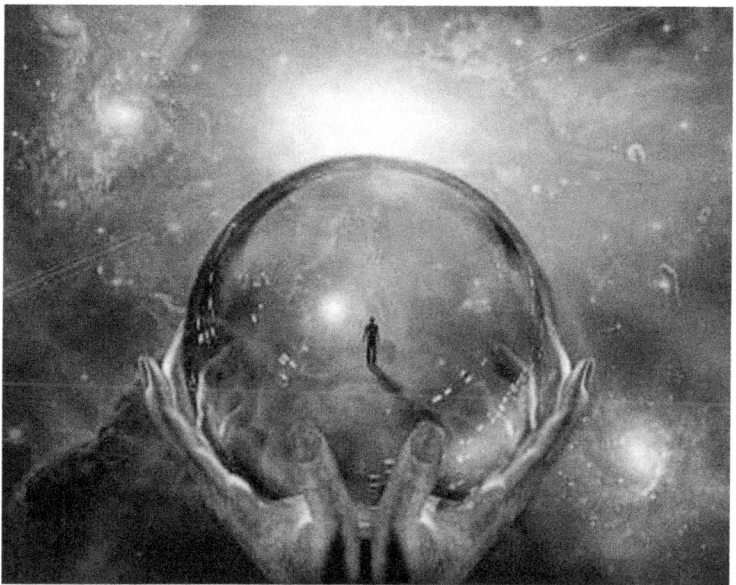

6. Awaken the Healer Within

The first law of Energy Medicine states, "disease occurs when there is an electrical imbalance in the auric field, the field of vibration that removes the blocking energy pattern is the cure". The Alchemist's Handbook to Homeopathy by Rev. Mary Hardy, Dotty Norman.

The word "Medicine" means to balance; to make whole, to heal the whole self; Body, Mind, Heart, and Soul. Holistic health is the ideal balance between all major parts of our being; body, mind, and soul in conjunction with our environment. The word healing comes from the Greek word "holos", whole, or Holistic healing is wholeness and encompasses our whole life. The intention for the individual must be to understand his or her own basic health patterns. All Paths of Spiritual Development teach us to look within, all healing and all answers come from looking within our self. Healing can be initiated from an outside source which serves to set the healing process in motion.

The call to wholeness begins with understanding how our emotional and spiritual health impacts our physical vitality. Many of the alternative theories help us to create a Holistic approach to healing that applies ancient healing practices with modern circumstances. Holistic therapies facilitate the healing of the whole person, Body, Mind, and Spirit, and attempt to stimulate the body's natural healing abilities. Holistic therapies help us find a root of a condition rather than just treating the symptoms. The Holistic approach seeks to understand how our body Mind and Spirit works together. Inner imbalances may be caused by toxic overload and mental, emotional, or spiritual blocks. When we hear the call to wholeness we may choose to heal our life by seeking a spiritual connection to our higher self. Aligning ourselves with spiritual truth raises the vibration and brings the whole organism into the Light where optimum health and healing can result.

We are metaphysical multi-dimensional beings, we operate from physical, emotional, mental, and spiritual dimensions simultaneously. For true healing to occur, we begin to learn how these dimensions all interact and affect our overall health. The word metaphysics means beyond physical awareness. Our chakras are our connection to this universe. the word chakra means disc. These disks of energy are vortices that extend out from the central nerves of our spinal column. Psychologically, our chakras relate to areas of our lives. Balancing & healing the major chakras can be done through a combination of energy or vibrational healing practices. When we have communication between the subtle bodies, vibrating as a unified whole, we have optimum health and well-being.

Alchemy, also called Vibrational Healing, is a secret of Ascension. We are multi-dimensional beings existing in a multi- dimensional Universe. Dis-ease occurs when we forget our connection with our Creator; for healing to occur, we must reestablish this Divine connection. In this way, we combine all Dimensions so that a complete healing can take place. Shamans are also Vibrational Practitioners who consider the whole person; seeing beyond the physical body into the realm of the electromagnetic energy structures, or subtle bodies. These bodies are called emotional, mental, causal, Astro, and the higher spiritual bodies.

Energy patterns or wave signatures are the method for changing the patterns in the subtle bodies. In vibrational healing we perceive everything as energy patterns. We see greater wholeness and look in the higher subtle bodies for the cause of the imbalance rather than to address only the physical body. To ascend into higher dimensions, we must work consciously with our subtle bodies. When we have identified and released certain blockages or removed disharmonious energy patterns in our beliefs, we will begin to integrate our energies. This will allow us to raise our vibratory rate so that we can ascend into the higher dimensions. It is in integrating our unique vibratory patterns and claiming our divine blueprint, that we will align our energies becoming One with our Creator.

Energy Medicine or Vibrational Medicine is a Holistic approach to healing your whole self; body, mind, heart, and soul. I work to address the emotional life trauma, to release and restore you through Soul Retrieval, Past Life and Future Regression, Shamanic Healing with Sound, and vibration. I will put you in an energy cocoon, where you release the old program that is not serving your highest good. Working with guides, to cut the cords of discord and dis-harmony that cause self-defeating patterns, you will be rewired with the new divine blueprint. Rising out of the cocoon, you will be reborn, a new being. The time of transfiguration and rebirth is now. Your new Light body is created from above and a new vibration formed from 5 new colors. Working with the Golden Light, your will be filled with Light vibration, assisting you on your journey to fulfill your Sacred Destiny in service to the Earth and Creation.

Clearing Emotional Blocks

The Shaman uses your subconscious mind to clear cellular memory. Shamanism is a journey to wholeness; clearing and healing emotional blockages created by past negative experiences, unresolved emotions, self-defeating behaviors or patterns and self-limiting beliefs that contribute to self-sabotage. They act as a defense mechanism to deal with deep emotional pain experienced in traumatic, destructive, and dysfunctional situations ranging from the loss of a loved one, betrayal, abuse, rejection, abandonment and more.

Emotional blockages manifest in your life when unfelt or suppressed emotions like anger, resentment, and guilt that are dense emotions, block your energy. The emotional body is magnetic and holds on to suppressed emotions until you allow them to move, by expressing them. Unless released these emotions hinder you from raising your vibrational frequencies and can result in physical manifestations like chronic pain, anxiety, migraines, ulcers, and other forms of illness. A healthy emotional body vibrates and attracts light, which is what raises consciousness.

'Triggers' activate undesirable feelings like anger, fear, hurt, sadness etc. from past experiences that have been repressed. You may be triggered by a person, a situation, song, smell, color, and more. For instance, when triggered by anger you may deflect your feelings and blame another or the situation. When you react to a trigger, it is a fear-based reaction and fear has a low vibrational frequency. Most often people react in anger even if what they feel is fear; they do this to protect themselves from feeling hurt. For most people anger becomes the primary defense mechanism. It is necessary to move anger (and other negative emotions), a dense energy out of your physical and emotional body to attract positive experiences.

Emotional blocks can affect all areas of life; relationships, finance, career, health, and more. In relationship issues, as a child, if your closest companion was your grandmother who was kind, loving, and affectionate and was the only one that made you feel safe and secure, the loss of that relationship creates feelings of loneliness, insecurity, abandonment, and grief. These associated feelings are implanted in the subconscious and manifest later in life hindering the development of close, intimate, relationships. This is a defense mechanism against the fear of reliving the pain of loss.

Cellular memory stores every experience we have had. Each cell in our body stores DNA which is passed down through generations. Just as the cells store biological DNA, they also store mental, emotional and spiritual levels. It is impossible for the conscious mind to remember every experience, but the memory of every experience is encoded in our cells. This is referred to as cellular memory. Traumatic incidents, from childhood or even past-lives can leave an emotional imprint on our cellular memory. For example, a person who has a fear of dogs may have experienced something traumatic that caused the fear. The shock/pain of the incident gets locked in their cellular memory even after the conscious mind forgets about the incident. The result is a 'deep-rooted fear'.

Swiss therapist Anne Miller having worked with patients who had suffered abuse as children concluded that suppressed emotions lead to problems such as depression, anger, abuse, and more. Blocking or repressing emotions, especially negative emotions result in a negative manifestation that can be destructive to you and those around you. By honestly allowing yourself to feel and release these emotions, you release the pain and trauma associated with it freeing yourself to live beyond pain and suffering.

7. Holly's Story

I met Holly at my Thursday night meditation meetup. It was a new experience for her to join a meditation group and to meditate. Drawn by the relaxation found in Yoga Breathing and the meditation itself, she wasn't expecting anything beyond and was doubtful anything further could help her. She was a recluse; getting on in years, showed signs she lived alone and had been a loner for years. She had successfully raised her daughter and was happy with her simple life. However, something drew her to the Meditation.

Blocked from going on the Soul Retrieval journey by her ego, she was happy to make a friend and learn relaxation from meditation. In fact, she met another woman who had a similar lifestyle, the two became friends.

Two weeks later, Holly sent me a letter explaining her life situation and her feelings. Her feelings poured out on the paper, expressing her pain in relationships that had gone bad, and her decision to be a hermit. She enjoyed nature and was happy with her garden. Yet, she wondered if there was more? She made an appointment for a Shamanic Healing Session.

Creating Sacred Space, I began to cleanse, clear, heal and seal her Chakras. Leading her in a gentle meditation, I asked her to imagine a beautiful flower opening in each chakra. Then placing her in an energy cocoon of gossamer threads, she was in the safe space to release her wounded past. I used sage and aromatherapy, cleansing and clearing, cutting cords with the past, blessing and healing her broken heart. I asked her to imagine that she has a new heart.

Journeying to the Chamber of Gifts, she was given the gift of Joy and love. She had felt unloved all her life, but now she was given a new heart and a new beginning. Looking ahead to a possible destiny, Holly saw herself giving flowers to people in nursing homes. In this way, she was told she is giving love to people who may feel unloved. And that as she gave love, she would receive love and Joy.

Holly was speechless, and excited. She saw her Self, self-realized. Perhaps her highest reality, and that it was attainable. One flower at a time, as she gives love, so she receives love. Looking at her composure, Holly appeared a new being, she was radiating. Not only had she released the pain and trauma of her past, but through healing and entering the Light, she embraced a bright new future.

I ended the session, detaching from our Spirit guides, I gave thanks for being a part of this healing session

8. Shamanism

In Shamanism, Journeying takes you on a journey to view your shadow self and integrate with your Soul Light. You journey into the Light in the heart of the world where you find your life purpose. Worlds open as you leave ordinary reality and journey to spiritual realms, embracing the Light; discovering your gifts, spirit guides, spirit animals, and life meaning.

The Shaman first creates sacred space, then begins Drumming the Heartbeat of Mother Earth. Setting your intention, you enter spiritual states of consciousness to view your wound that caused the original Trauma. Then you can begin the healing journey in search of your life meaning. Shamans bring awareness of the interconnectedness of all life and a return to relationship with the Earth. Medicine Wheel teachings show this interconnection and teach the Law of One and all our Medicine helpers. Indigenous Elders speak of our present world of separation as an illusion that is collapsing because it doesn't serve the whole. As we transform our thoughts, words, and deeds to be inclusive of the whole, we expand our worldview. As we put our minds together as one, drawing from ancient wisdom, we align with the Divine Plan for good for the Earth and her People.

We have experienced environmental degradation since our shift in consciousness causing separation from nature resulting in imbalance and entropy. Human beings are faced with the option to preserve nature and learn from our indigenous Elders how to breathe new life into the planet or to continue the path of certain destruction. The two are innately interconnected, what happens to the Earth, happens to Man. We are not separate from the Earth and Creation, we are Spiritual beings and we are the Earth, we are born to rise, to evolve beyond this present darkness. Shaman's have a Vision of a New Earth that we are collectively seeding to bring forth new life, a new beginning for humankind, a new frontier of consciousness blossoming. This field is ready for planting the original seed and Divine blueprint of the Consciousness of One. When we put our minds together as ONE with Creator and collectively hold the vision, we are creating the new beginning. What is your vision, how do you imagine the new Earth?

Shamanism is a growth experience, a spiritual journey in search of your true self. You start with the question, Who am I? Why am I here? How can I serve the whole? A Shaman enters alternate dimensions to rebalance a client's mind, body, and spirit connection and to retrieve fragments of the soul lost to emotional, mental, or physical trauma. To be a Shaman, you experience healing yourself, then through spiritual initiations opening lines of communication with Creator, your Spiritual Guides, Spirit Animals, and your personal Vision, you follow the Path revealing your Truth. When you are ready to heal, and have passion to heal others, you begin the Journey of self-realization and fulfilling your Sacred Destiny.

You become One with the Earth as you give gratitude and acknowledgment to the Earth for all the gifts she gives us: Air, Water, Fire, and the Earth herself from which we are made. Send positive energy to her, feel her energy, feel the Earth beneath your feet and realize she supports all life. Walk in bare feet to ground your energy and be one with the Earth. Spend time in Nature every day, open awareness of the sounds, the birds; sights, the animals, trees, water; smells, smell the plants, the air; feel the wind on your face. Refresh your spirit as you become grounded, cleansing your Root Chakra. Becoming one with nature you feel the Earth and begin to learn about your energy and its patterns. The atmosphere around your body attracts people and situations to you. When you have negative thoughts, replace them with positive and compassionate images to attract loving energy. Shamans focus on manifesting a reality filled with love. In a reality filled with love, you will attract love into your world. That is the Law of Attraction. As man heals himself, he heals the world.

Healing begins within as you learn the patterns of imbalance within yourself. A Shaman guides her client with the sound of the Drum where you enter alternate spirit dimensions and begin your Spiritual Journey. You can learn to heal by looking deep within yourself, all answers are found within; you can journey on a personal Vision Quest, or the Soul Journey with a Shaman. Shamanism is built on experience; a will to heal yourself, and an openness to change as you experience initiations that serve to connect you with all worlds and other realities. The Shaman learns to walk between worlds and guides others into the Light.

Confronting fear of abandonment is one of the most difficult challenges you may face if you choose to go on your healing path, you may have to make choices; you can choose not to abandon your healing process and spiritual growth, or you can deny your need for change. When you choose not to abandon yourself, you begin weaving new patterns into your life experience that will support you in the forward movement and healing. But, if you abandon your inner knowing that calls for change, then you've woven threads into the dream weave that will present you with the lessons you need to learn about abandonment issues. You may have abandoned your personal integrity, your feelings, your sense of self-esteem, or your personal Creed. By abandoning yourself, you remain in the illusion of separation that causes imbalance, illness, and eventual entropy. Shaman's guide you to open awareness to your intuition, your sense of well-being, and inner knowing. When you acknowledge and honor your own patterns of dysfunction and illness, and are willing to surrender them, the alternate path that appears unexpectedly can urge you to grow beyond your former lifestyles and identities, aligning with new people who also honor you for who you are.

The Mayans use the onion to represent layers peeled away to reveal the Spiritual Essence of the healed human being. It is the courageous human who is willing to embrace the work required to strip away the layers needed to reach authentic freedom. You reach this kind of freedom when you see every challenge in life as an opportunity to heal, creating a bright strong courage, inner knowing, and Truth. You learn that the layers of the onion are peeled away as you embrace life with understanding that all experiences are valid initiations that give you the power of choice. That ability to discern allows you to choose how to relate to the events in your life and to move through the gates that these experiences open. You are presented with choices about believing a negative idea presented by the Shadow and miss the opportunity to heal by honoring your own free will. By choosing healing, you can replace the thought with a more positive one and call back your energy from investment in your own illness or dysfunction.

When you begin to grow Spiritually, you realize that everything you think, feel, dream, and all your actions, contain your life force. That energy is motivated by your intent and personal will, called your volition. The more aware you become of how you are investing your energy, the easier it becomes to reclaim that life force and channel it into areas that allow you to manifest the dreams held in your heart. Patterns of behavior that have leaked energy through negative ideas or critical feelings are the property of the Shadow and the realm of the shadow that can be healed.

Shamans are always attuned to symbols and messages found in nature. A favorite animal, or an animal that continues to cross your path, may be your spirit animal visiting you to bring you a message or to remind you of your strengths. You can research this animal's symbolic meaning and how it fits into your journey of spiritual growth.

The Vision Quest is a way to begin your understanding of who you are, how Spirit communicates with you. Spirit can bring messages through all of Nature to teach you the unity that can be found in all living things. Find a special place in Nature and create sacred space around you. Set the intention for Spirit to speak to you through the animals, birds, the trees. Enter the silence by opening awareness of all your senses. What sounds do you hear? What colors do you see? Now, allow your mind to relax and open to receiving divine messages from your spirit guides. Wait to see if an animal appears to you that may bring you a message.

9. Maria's Story

Maria came to me for a Soul Retrieval Session. When she came into the office she stated that she felt scared and confused. Her energy felt heavy, like weights on her shoulders. We began with the sound of the drum; the heartbeat of the Mother, leading her to relax; we followed the yoga breathing to relax her body, and mind, we proceeded.

She discovered her original wound happened when she was abused as a child; leading to feelings of insecurity, jealousy, doubt, sadness, and loneliness. She felt no one loved her, that she was alone in life, abandoned.

We journeyed to the chamber of Healing where I placed her inside the bright Golden Light, illuminating her shadow. Then proceeding with Shamanic Healing, I used the rattle to loosen energy as I pulled negative, blocked energy off her, cutting cords, and freeing her from the bondage of abuse and it's many symptoms.

Placing her in an energy cocoon, I wrapped her in gossamer threads of gold and silver Light. She released her old self; her wounded self that lived in the illusion of being unlovable, alone. Asking her to release all the old mental patterns that prevented her from reaching her higher self, that held her in limiting belief patterns of unworthiness; Maria shed the old self inside the invisible energy cocoon wrapped firmly around her. Rattles, essential oil, smudging with sage, and vibrational energy were applied during the process of release.

Becoming one with the Light and her higher self, I told her she was being rewired with a new divine blueprint from above. That we are born with an earthly body, but also receive a Light body from Spirit, becoming one with our Soul. She saw herself rising out of the cocoon with wings; feeling love, forgiveness, and trust, perhaps for the first time in her life. She said, "I feel giddy, joyful, completely energized. When I came into your office I felt heavy and sad and now I'm happy and filled with energy, I feel like dancing!"

"Soul Retrieval and Shamanic Healing with Caroline Dawley is a profound healing experience. I highly recommend her nurturing and healing services. I walked into her office feeling heavy and needed guidance. Caroline holds a compassionate and grounding energy and is a wonderful listener. The Healing session consisted of the Buffalo Drum beat playing while Caroline's soothing voice guided me to Chambers of Healing in deep meditation. Through my meditation, I had amazing revelations and messages that were beneficial to my well-being. I visited an old wound for clarity and healing and retrieved a part of my soul left behind from trauma. In meditation, I was in a cocoon of healing energy while Caroline gave me Reiki and Sound Healing, and I was reborn as a new soul. I now have clarity of my divine spirit and the beauty and grace that I am, (that we all are), separate from the illusion of the ego. Since the healing, I have been full of ecstatic and explosive energy. I felt like I had been carrying a weight around with me, which was my deep-seated wound, and now I feel light as a feather. I feel full of unconditional love, enthusiasm, abundance, joy, faith, and security. I highly recommend going to see Caroline for a healing session. Her presence and gifts changed my life forever, for the better".

Maria

10. Soul Retrieval – What is It?

"Shamans understand that a piece of the soul leaves the body and goes to a territory in what shamans call non-ordinary reality where it waits until someone intervenes in the spiritual realms and facilitates its return. Although soul loss is a survival mechanism from a shamanic point of view, the soul part that left usually does not come back on its own. The soul might be lost, or stolen by another person, or doesn't know the trauma has passed and it is safe to return".

Alberto Villoldo

The benefits of having a Soul Retrieval are powerful experiences of healing. In Soul Retrieval we address symptoms of Trauma; anxiety, PTSD, feelings of abandonment, feeling lost, emotional dysfunction. In Soul Retrieval the intent is to reclaim your lost soul part and integrate with the Light, freeing you to find life's meaning. Soul Retrieval helps you take control of your emotions and teaches you how to journey beyond the illusion of ordinary life. You learn how to work with the Oneness of life, with your Spirit animals, Spirit guides, allies and Creator. Soul Retrieval helps you answer the call to be whole, to reclaim your life purpose and begin your Journey to your Sacred Destiny. Soul Retrieval is the beginning of your healing journey in search of their true Self. For some, the entire composure of their body changes, they say, "I feel like I came home to myself". Or "I am completely changed, or that's exactly what I needed!"

There are many symptoms of soul loss. Some of the more common ones would be trauma caused from war, dissociation from the body after an operation or car accident, from sexual abuse, or abandonment and the person says, "I don't feel I am fully in my body". Other symptoms include anxiety, depression, suicidal tendencies, post-traumatic stress disorder, grief, addictions. Addictions are also a sign of soul loss as you seek external sources to self-medicate and dull your pain. Anytime someone says, "I have never been the same" since a certain event, soul loss has probably occurred. Many times, a veteran returning from war will say, "I feel like part of myself is still on the field".

The Shaman enters into a Spiritual Ceremony with their client during a Soul Retrieval. First creating Sacred Space, the Shaman invokes the four directions and personal guides before beginning the journey that guides her client into an altered state of consciousness. Setting the intention, and singing the Power Song, we begin drumming. Journeying beyond ordinary reality, I use vision and intuitive guidance to direct them. Through years of building spiritual connections with my allies; I work with my Spirit Animals, with the Elements, my personal Spiritual Guides, and Vision, to know the way into the other worlds and safely return with the information being sought.

The intention for Healing is for the highest and greatest good for the client. Then stating the intention for the Journey, the Shaman guides the client into the underworld where they first repair any wound that is found with the Mother. Sometimes, if there is resistance and the client is unable to reestablish this union with Mother Earth, then the Shaman knows to travel to find the Mother Wound.

The Soul Retrieval may take a few sessions to complete the Journey from finding the Wound, healing it, meeting the Healed Soul, and reintegrating it with their client. Shamanic Healing is the method I use to cleanse, clear, heal and seal the wound and prepare for integration with the Soul. During this session, smudging with sage, I first use my Wing to cleanse away any negative energy in and around the Aura. I use Reiki and Vibrational energy healing to cleanse and clear, and a

Rattle to break up the energy blockages. Then working closely with the element Fire for Purification, I ask the client to visualize they are inhaling Golden Liquid Light through the top of their head, all the way down through their body down into the Earth. Healing every cell and tissue, every organ, with Healing Light that is Purifying their whole body. During this session the client may comment that they feel me pulling energy from their body that is being released because it is not serving their higher good. Other people comment that trauma and pain are flying off their body, sometimes their legs vibrate as energy is released. Then I teach them to visualize they are sitting in the Center of the Sun, surrounded with Golden Light, transmuting and transforming into a higher energy vibration.

Next, I put them in an energy cocoon that is woven with gossamer threads of silver and gold. Asking them to consciously release their old form, while being rewired with their Divine Blueprint. Imagining each chakra opening as a beautiful flower, they are transformed as they imagine themselves rising, leaving behind the old form, they put on their new Lightbody. Many exclaim afterward, "I feel brand new." Others say, "I have wings", others say, "I have a new heart!"

After the Soul Retrieval and Shamanic Healing, we journey to discover their healed Soul that is waiting for them. Almost everyone is able to see their Soul, the approximate age, and to ask it if she or he will return with them. Some Souls give instructions on what the client needs to do before the Soul can integrate. One of my clients commented that they needed to be humble, for another, she needed to be less critical of herself, for another, she needed to meditate and change her lifestyle. However, there were some who integrated with their Soul easily, and when asking what gift, she or he brings, the soul comments were, "I bring you Joy", and another, "I am your Life Essence", when asked what happens if we don't integrate? The soul replied, "without me you will die". And another, "I am the Light of your Life". The Soul is then invited to integrate with my client and instructions are given them to continue integrating their relationship so that they will become one. When they become One, they begin to be Soul directed instead of ego directed and begin to raise awareness of the interconnection with the divine.

It has always been the role of the Shaman to go into an altered state of consciousness and find where the soul went in the alternate realities and return it to the body of the client. My power to enter different realities comes from my Winged helpers from the Bird Tribe. Raven helps me teach clients how to fly into the Dark Night of the Soul and find the Light inside. Eagle gives me Vision to see from a higher perspective, the Iroquois refer to as "the High Mind of Creator". I call on Eagle to escort us to the upper world where my client learns Eagle Medicine and how to see from a higher point of view. Where they may see a vision of their Sacred Destiny.

The return of the lost Soul is the beginning of being One with Spirit, with Creator and the Whole of Creation. It is the beginning of the Spiritual Journey of discovering you Authentic Self and all the gifts you were born with that will assist you to reach your Destiny.

Today, we live in the world of illusion and duality, I call the Shadow World. We can see how imbalanced the Earth and all Creation is as we see the amount of illness in society and in our environment. The fragmentation of the Soul causes the Shadow World to control our lives. As the Earth spins farther and farther out of balance, more and more animals will become extinct, more trees will be logged or die from contamination and lack of respect for our environment. The Sea becomes toxic from waste and neglect, and man refuses to be Stewards of the Earth. At the United Nations "Cry of the Earth" Summit in 1993, I heard firsthand the prophecies for the Earth from the Indigenous First Peoples Nations, who came from the Four Directions. I was sickened as I listened to the disheartening prophecies that were spoken about the Great Change on Earth, and that "the Earth will end as we know it if man does not change". Chief Shenandoah, Iroquois

Soul Retrieval is a Spiritual Practice for healing the original wound caused from Man's Fall from Grace; and the resulting Trauma caused from his separation from the Earth Mother and Creator. When the Worldview of Duality Consciousness and separation is healed, and

Man opens awareness of the interconnection of all parts as one evolving Whole, he becomes One with his Soul Light and ascends to a higher reality. When you become Soul Directed, you take your place as One People working to heal Mankind and the Earth. The Shaman sees beyond this present darkness into the Light of the New Earth. My task is to teach people how to fly into the Light and be one with Spirit that lives in all things, illuminating the shadow. We are born to remember who we are and evolve beyond this cycle of birth, death, rebirth, to the New Earth, the Iroquois call, The Fifth World of Peace and illumination. A ho.

11. Shamanic Healing with Sound

To practice Shamanic Healing, we form a sacred circle and cleanse with the sacred sage, creating Sacred Space. While listening to the sound of the drum in a guided meditation, those gathered journey outside of time where they are led to a healing space called their secret garden. Then the Shaman uses sounds; drumming and rattles to shake up the blocked energy. When there has been a traumatic event, energy becomes stuck in the energy bodies of the participant, rattles and drums release this trauma. The Shaman uses smoke from the sage to clear away the negative energy. Then using a drum, rattle, bells, singing bowl, and different sounds to break up stuck energy and clear the chakras. Sometimes pulling psychic energy in the form of energetic poison darts from the energy field. Many times, the client vibrates as the clearing takes place and energy is replaced. The client feels restored to wellbeing. The space is again cleared of all negative energy.

In shamanic healing, we use sound for spiritual atonement and to aid in the process of awakening to the powerful forces of nature. The shaman uses rituals and tools to align with the energies and powers of nature and manifest them in his or her life. Shaman's tools are the drum, beating out the rhythm of life that affects all physical energies. The rhythm represents the heartbeat of Mother Earth; the rattle and rhythmic sounds break up the rigid energy patterns around the body, promoting healing and balance and helps break up congestion or energy blockages. For healing, shake the rattle around the aura of the body and then run down the front and the back of the body. Finish by smudging the aura and intend that negative energy will be escorted away.

Shamans can use the voice in a spirit language to commune with higher intelligences to extract proper remedies. Some Indians believe that consciousness emits a high frequency hissing or whistling noise. Many shamans use their voice as the divine instrument, singing their medicine song or some form of directed esoteric toning. For myself, I choose to sing an Algonquin Healing Song, and I use the wind to assist transformation and healing. Listening to the rhythm of the Drum opens consciousness to entering other realms and journeying in search of answers to our life. When we set the intention, then journey to the heartbeat of the Drum, all the answers can be found inside.

In Shamanism we seek to clear our emotional body, our mental body, and drop density in our physical body. By mastering our emotions and mental patterns, we will become masters of our body as we integrate all three bodies, we will become one with our Soul.

Traumatic events from the past live in the body as blocked energy, unaddressed emotional trauma lives in our cells as cell memory and predispose our bodies to illness or dis-ease. Emotional body clearing is the process of releasing the blocks and illuminating the shadow, raising the vibration, and healing. Traumatic events may also live in the mental body in the form of fears, phobias, limiting patterns of thinking, where they live in the subconscious mind and continue to control our life. Through Soul Journeying you can connect with your higher mind, with the Light, where you raise awareness and release patterns that keep you bound in lower vibrational patterns of dysfunction and illness. You create your reality with your thoughts, you are what you think. Shamanic healing offers mental body clearing through illuminating your mind with Truth, freeing you from limiting points of view and expanding awareness of the whole. Through Soul Retrieval, you become masters of your mind and emotions. What you do not heal will manifest in the body as dis-ease. Shamanism helps you raise the frequency of the inner Light, becoming One with your Soul, you integrate Mind, Body, and Spirit. You now realize your Divine Self.

Native Americans and Shamans learn how to access all dimensions, traveling inter-dimensionally, we enter worlds within worlds. The Medicine Wheel is a tool to help us experience the interconnectedness of all life so that we walk in balance and harmony with all our relations who share our beautiful planet.

12. Create Sacred Space

On our first journey, while following the sound of the drum, we Journey to the lower world to visit a Sacred Garden in the womb of Mother Earth. In this realm, we heal our relationship with Mother Earth, our Mother whom we have never been separated from.

To create sacred space, first find a place where you feel very comfortable and begin to call in the four directions which protect you putting you in an invisible energy circle. The four directions and energies place you in relationship with all life, the ancient, and all of creation. The Iroquois call them the "protectors" and spirit keepers of the four directions or gates. As you commune with those forces from the ground of Sacred Space you are protected and the principles of the four directions and the universe respond. I use Alberto Villoldo's form for opening sacred space because it teaches each person how to prepare themselves. To open Sacred Space, close your eyes and move your hands into a prayerful pose at your heart extending your arms up with intention, past your forehead so that they come together above your head then reach up to your 8th chakra which is the soul chakra and expand this radiant sun to cover your entire body. Then fan your arms out to your side bringing your hands to rest in your lap.

Another way to open sacred space is by facing each direction as you call to the four cardinal directions; south, west, north, and east as well as to Heaven and Earth and ask them to assist you and protect you.

Each point of this circle is governed by an animal; in the south we call to Wolf who represents our teacher and pathfinder. In the west, we call on grandmother bear who teaches us how to go within and find all the answers deep within ourselves. Who leads us into the cave and symbolizes strength and courage to enter the void without fear. In the north, the Ancestors guide us and send us wisdom, in the east we call on eagle who symbolizes the ability to transcend this world. Above, we call on Heaven and the life-sustaining Sun, and below us, we call on the Earth, our Mother.

This is the prayer to bring about Sacred Space: to the winds of the south, I call on Wolf to teach me to find the path and follow the path, to walk softly on the earth, teach me the beauty way. Thank you, Wolf, for helping me follow the path.

To the Winds of the West I call on Grandmother Bear to protect my Sacred Space and teach me the way of Peace, show me the way beyond time, the way of transformation; thank you Grandmother for giving me courage to enter the void. To the Winds of the North, I call on the grandmothers and grandfathers, the Ancient Ones; come and warm your hands by our fires, whisper to me words of wisdom, I honor you who have come before me and those who will come after me. To the Winds of the East; Eagle come to me from the place of the rising Sun, helping me see with the high mind of Creator, teach me to fly wing to wing with the Great Spirit, to see with eyes of the heart. Mother Earth, I pray for healing for all your children, all my relations; thank you for the Sun that rises daily, for Grandmother Moon and the Star Nations. Great Spirit, thank you for giving me one more day to walk upon the Earth.

Relax and be comfortable, now I want you to begin breathing to the count of seven, begin to inhale bringing that beautiful Light above your head down into your body and hold your breath to the count of 7, and then releasing your breath to the count of 7, just exhale all anxiety all tension and just feel your body relaxing, more and more with every breath you feel lighter and lighter. Now open awareness to the sound of the drum, drumming the heartbeat of Mother Earth. Align with the energies of the Divine Mother and the Heavenly Father, and Great Mystery within.

13. Mary's Story

I met Mary at my Thursday night Meditation Meetup and afterward she signed up for a private appointment. When we met in my office, she said she suffered from Trauma caused when her daughter almost died during a boating accident, and that she had lost two fingers. She had experienced a lot of trauma with her other daughter also and was experiencing anxiety and PTSD.

During our Soul Retrieval journey, Mary journeyed to her original wound that caused trauma, anxiety, and unhappiness in her life. In the chamber of healing, I placed her inside the Bright Golden Light and asked her to breathe this Light into every cell in her body. To become one with this Light. Then, she released her emotions that had been blocked, she said she felt old energy being pulled out of her throat chakra, that caused her to lose her ability to write and express her feelings creatively. She saw each blocked emotion released, being transmuted to a higher vibration as she received more and more Light into her being.

Journeying to the Chamber of Gifts and Treasures, Mary found a pen, a feather, and a book that she picked up and breathed into her energy field. These gifts symbolize her latent ability to write a book telling the true story of her healing journey. In the upper world, where she met her celestial guides she was told, "by telling her story she will help others have the strength and courage to heal".

Mary returned for another Session the following week and asked to have a Past Life Regression with the intention of "finding her soulmate or love of her life". In the regression, I led Mary in a relaxation exercise with yoga breathing and a guided journey into her Sacred Garden. Setting the intention for her guide to show her a life where she shared a happy relationship with a man who could be her soulmate. Immediately, she saw herself with a man and said they were married and very much in love. She learned his name was Justin, and described him, saying she was very happy with him. During her life review she said, "He was the love of my life".

In the next part of the regression, spirit directed me to guide her into the future with the intention of finding her soulmate, or true love. I was surprised at the instruction but proceeded as advised. Leading Mary on a journey to her Sacred Garden, I then led her to a place in the future where she saw herself meeting a man. I asked her where she was when they met. She said, we were at St. Petersburg beach at a festival and he walked up to her. She described him as the same man she had known in the past life, only his hair was darker. She said he asked her to go out with him. She said she was certain he was the same man". Guiding her forward, I asked if they were still dating and she replied that he had invited her to a baseball game. Then she said, "he asked me to marry him, and I said, yes". She said he lived in a large house overlooking the Gulf and she was going to have a wonderful life with the man of her dreams, the love of her life. She said, "I'm very happy! I'm elated"!

I disconnected from our many spirit guides and gave thanks for being a part of this healing session.

14. Animal Totems and Their Significance

From his book, Animal Speak, Ted Andrews said, "If you talk to the animals they will talk with you and you will know each other. If you do not talk to them, you will not know them and what you do not know you will fear; what one fears one destroys."

When any animal presents itself to you in some way that stands out in your mind, whether in a dream or while you are awake; study it, it has a message for you. In the east; The animal of the east guides you to your greatest spiritual challenges and guards your path to spiritual awakening. Eagle, brings gifts of clarity, vision, and new beginnings.

The animal of the South protects the child within and reminds you when to be humble and when to trust, so that innocence will be balanced in your personality. Wolf is a teacher and protector who guides you to find the Heart Path where you learn loyalty and unconditional love for yourself and others, where you purify your heart in the eternal flame of love. The animal in the West leads you to your personal truth and inner answers. It also shows you the path to your goals. Grandmother Bear gives you courage to go within to find your spiritual truth.

The animal of the North gives wise counsel and reminds you when to speak and when to listen. It also reminds you to be grateful for every blessing every day. White Buffalo teaches the Medicine Wheel and its wisdom, by teaching that when you give in the circle of life, you receive everything you need. The above direction animal teaches you how to honor the Great Star Nation and reminds you that you came from the stars and to the stars you will return. This animal is also the guardian of the dreamtime and for your personal access to the other dimensions.

The below direction animal teaches you about the inner Earth, and how to stay grounded and on the path. The within animal teaches you how to find your heart's joy and how to be faithful to your personal truths. It is also the protector of your sacred space, the place that is yours, and is never shared except by invitation.

To discover your totem animals, ask this question, what animals were you seeing when you were a child? What animals fascinate you now? Do you dream of certain animals? What animal most frightens you, or makes you feel uncomfortable? One way to identify your totem animal or power animal is to keep a journal of what animal you see regularly or is the first animal that you see in the morning. Since the aura reflects the animal of the individual; what animal does your aura reflect, what animal reflects your posture and body movement? Spiritual perception of the totem through a Spirit Guide May confirm an animal totem. The Iroquois Wisdom Wheel of Transformation teaches that we each receive the gift of a totem animal at birth depending on the Moon cycle we are born under.

Native Americans believe that each animal is a messenger, they are our teachers. Animals are conscious, sentient beings and it is important that we treat all living creatures with dignity and respect. The ancients have always regarded animals as being sacred and their behavior can teach us how to enter the world of nature and become one with our environment. It's up to the Shaman to assist in interpreting the symbols and messages of the animals and creatures of the forest, but with practice you can lean to communicate with the animals. By watching the behavior of animals, we can get a better understanding of the energy around us and a deeper insight into intuitive messages and signs. Spirit animals are similar to our spiritual guides, who come into our lives to give us a message or to teach us something about our own ability and strength. Sometimes an animal will come into our lives for a brief period of time as a way to signal us to something that we need to pay attention to.

Hawk: The strong hawk has keen eyes and strong wings. If you continually see hawks or images of hawks, it may be a sign that you need to look at something more closely before proceeding. It may also be a sign that a strong or important teacher or lesson will be unfolding in your life shortly. Many times, Hawk is a messenger.

Eagle: The eagle is a sign of spiritual protection and moving to a level of higher consciousness. If you repeatedly see eagles or eagle imagery in your life, it could be that you are transcending or shifting into a new realm of consciousness, giving you the ability to see from a higher perspective.

Raven and Crow: Commonly considered a bad omen, seeing a crow or raven could indicate that you are ready to let go of something or that you are getting ready to enter a "death and rebirth" cycle. Raven can be a sign that you are about to enter a new dimension of understanding. Seeing a raven or crow very rarely indicates physical death, instead it is a sign of an upcoming rebirth.

Owl: Seeing an owl is an indicator that you need to pay attention to your intuition and wisdom. The owl also comes as a reminder to pay attention to any gut feelings that you may be receiving as they are trying to point you in the right direction. The owl may also be a sign that you need to tune into your truth and act from a place of authenticity. Some people believe that if an owl makes a significance appearance in your life, they may be telling you that someone is ready to cross over. It doesn't mean it will happen, but there is a possibility.

Cardinal: Cardinal birds have often been associated with receiving a message from a deceased father figure or a male spirit guide. If you repeatedly see cardinals it could be a reminder that you are being loved and protected by this male, or a reminder to stay strong and confident in the path that you are walking.

Blue Jay: Seeing a Blue Jay is often associated with receiving a message from a deceased female figure or female spirit guide. If you repeatedly see Blue Jays, it may be a reminder to tune into your creativity and keep your creative projects flowing. It could also be an indication that your family needs you or that family unity is important.

Praying Mantis: The praying mantis comes to remind us that it is time to bring peace and stillness into our lives. The praying mantis comes as a messenger to remind us about the power of stillness and creating space in our lives for the things that we enjoy doing. Seeing a praying mantis repeatedly may also be a sign that there is a message that you need to pay attention to or something that you may be missing. Lizard: If you repeatedly see lizards or lizard imagery, it may be an indicator that you need to pay more attention to your dreams and goals. Perhaps you have lost sight of all that you can achieve or perhaps you are feeling negative about your abilities to achieve all that you desire. Seeing a lizard is a reminder that you do have the power and that you need to spend more time cultivating your highest path.

Snake: Seeing a snake is a powerful reminder of your life force and your passions. If you repeatedly see snakes or imagery of snakes, it could be that you need to pay attention to your passions and put more energy into pursuing them. Seeing a snake may also indicate that you are entering a place of healing and renewal.

Spider: Spiders carry powerful symbolism about creation and spiritual connectedness. When you see spiders often it may be an indication that you need to tune into your creative potential and follow through on any ideas or inspirations that you have to create. It may also be a sign of your connectedness to the spirit world and perhaps also indicate that spirit is trying to send you a message or reminder about this connection.

Dragonfly: Seeing a dragonfly is a reminder that you are not alone and that you are very protected by your guardian angels and spirit guides. If you repeatedly see dragonflies it may also indicate that you are on the right path and are heading in the right direction for your soul. Ladybug: The ladybug is commonly seen as a good luck sign and indicates that things are about to shift in your favor. Seeing ladybugs or ladybug imagery repeatedly may also be a sign of your need to pay gratitude for all that you have and the direction that your life is taking.

Ladybugs may also indicate a good time for you to push forward in obtaining your highest dreams and wishes.

<u>Butterfly</u>: Butterflies come to remind you about the power of transformation and that there needs to be a shift internally before you can shift externally. If you are repeatedly seeing butterflies, it may be a sign that you need to change or release some thoughts or feelings that are holding you back. Seeing a butterfly may also indicate a cycle of transformation or growth occurring in your life.

<u>Wolf</u>: Repeatedly seeing a wolf or imagery of a wolf may indicate that it is time for you to pay attention to the people you are surrounding yourself with. If you see a wolf, it is perhaps also a sign that you need to learn how to accept help from others, or to be more gregarious.

<u>Fox</u>: Fox comes as a reminder that there could be a different way for you to approach your life or see things. If you repeatedly see foxes or imagery of foxes, it could be that you need to adjust your thinking about something and the way you are approaching things. Start by observing and blending into nature, fox is good at camouflage. Fox may also come as a reminder to seek joy, to not take things so seriously and to laugh at the little things. Using your intuition will be key in determining what messages an animal is trying to bring into your life.

When we regularly go into nature, we open ourselves to the supernatural realms where Creator can communicate with us in a sacred way. When we set our intention, first ask for signs and communication from nature; meditate near a stream or body of water, become one with the water. Meditate in a grove of trees or sit beneath the trees, open your senses, and imagine that you are a part of the environment and that you are one with all Creation.

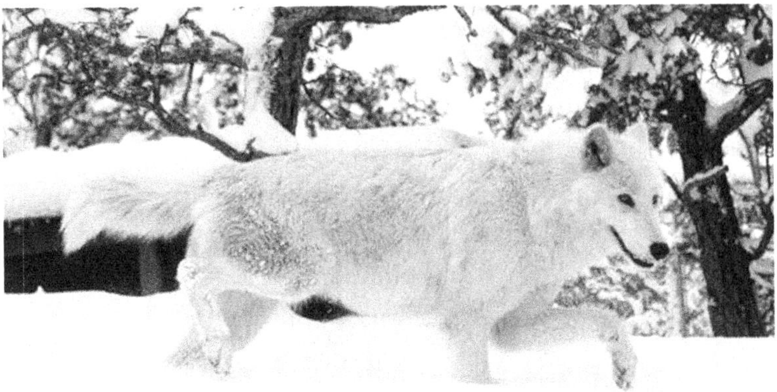

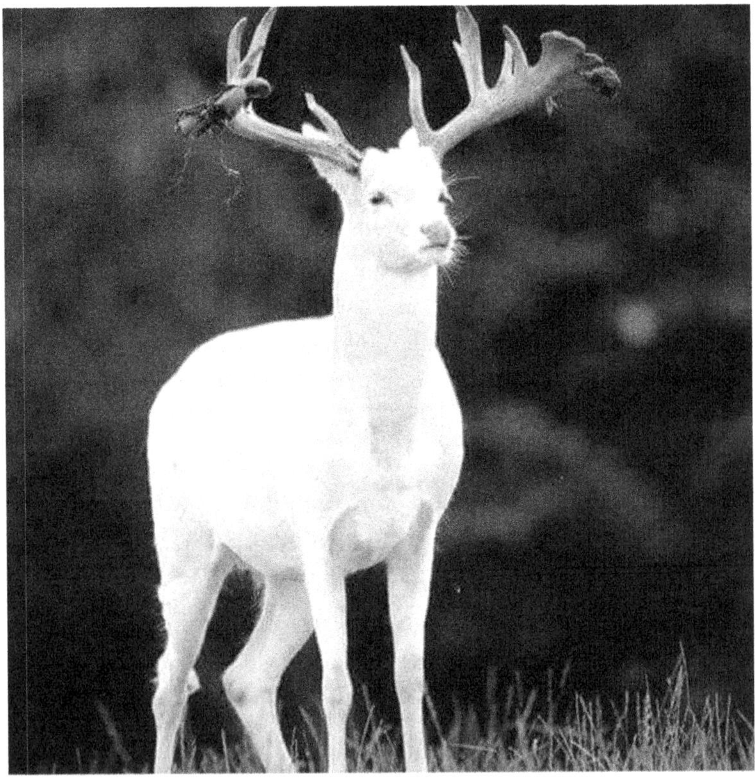

15. Journey to Retrieve Your Spirit Animals

Even the smallest most ordinary animal can be a wise instructor; all animals have lessons for us to learn and gifts for us to receive. Native Americans have always been one with nature and the natural world; by getting to know the animals you realize the animals are teachers and messengers helping us in our life Journey. There are four spirit keeper animals of North America.

Wolf is the pathfinder and star-walker, spiritual guide, and teacher who helps us find our path and follow our path. Bear teaches us how to go within in meditation and prayer into the inner Journey where we find the answers to our questions; giving us strength and courage for our journey. Buffalo teaches us how to give everything, in order to gain everything, and teaches us the circle of life that continues giving. What we receive in return may be from someone else, but Buffalo is a gift; Buffalo comes to give us wisdom for our journey.

Eagle is a powerful spirit keeper that symbolizes clarity and vision. The shaman understands that Eagle energy helps us perceive our entire life without becoming a part of the drama. Eagle assists us by giving us energy to find the guiding vision of our lives and helps us look at the whole picture to understand both where we came from, where we're going, and who we're becoming. Eagle gives us Wings to soar to high peaks far above day-to-day struggles and gives us tremendous vision. Eagle represents the self, transcending the principle of nature. Your spirit animal has gifts to help you find your calling and fulfill your Destiny.

To Journey to retrieve your Spirit Animal; prepare for this journey by opening Sacred Space. Sit comfortably and just close your eyes take your hands into your prayer pose at your heart and voice your intention to get in touch with your spirit animal on this journey. When you open Sacred Space begin to breathe the little yoga breath as you journey to your sacred garden in the lower world where you will greet your guide and state your intent to meet your spirit animal.

When you meet your animal ally and you're ready to invite your animal to come back with you, take your leave from your guide, and call on your spirit animal to return with you. Reach out your hands and feel the energy of your power animal and then bring it to you, feel its energy infusing every cell in your body. Observe the animal, study the animal, become one with this animal. Learn the gifts it brings you. Ask your animal the right questions: what gift do you bring to me, what medicine are you teaching me? Are you my teacher? What are your strengths, your weaknesses? How will you help me in my healing? How long have you been with me? Thank your spirit animal for being your guide.

16. Cassie's Story

The following is Cassie's story that I recreated after her Soul Retrieval Journey. Cassie came to me suffering from grief and despair; she explained that her husband had died and left her with 4 small children to raise by herself, she was afraid and overwhelmed. Her sister suggested she have Soul Retrieval session to help relieve her grief. The following is the Story that evolved after her sessions, that I recreated from the symbols and from spirit intuition.

Cassie, the Bear is your Spirit Animal who walks with you and is here to guide you on your healing journey to wholeness. She has much to teach you and is your strong ally in times of difficulty.

In the kingdom of spirit animals, the bear is symbolic of grounding forces and strength. This animal has been worshiped throughout time as a powerful totem, inspiring those who need it with the courage to stand up against adversity. As a spirit animal in touch with the earth and the cycles of nature, it is a powerful guide to support physical and emotional healing.

The bear has several meanings that will inspire those who have this animal as totem:

•The primary meaning of the bear spirit animal is strength and confidence; standing against adversity, taking action, and leadership.

•The spirit of the bear indicates it's time for healing or using healing abilities to help yourself, then help others.

•The bear medicine emphasizes the importance of solitude, quiet time, rest.

The bear is a spirit animal symbolic of strength and courage. The spirit of the bear is a strong source of support in times of difficulty. It provides courage and a stable foundation to face challenges. When the bear shows up as a spirit guide in your life, it's perhaps time to stand for your beliefs or your truth. This power animal will provide both support and strength.

The bear is also a guide to help you take leadership in your life and to guide your children. This animal is feared and admired for its strength. Its presence inspires respect. Its strength and powerful stature will inspire you to step into a leadership role in your life and take action without fear. When you invoke the power of the bear totem, reflect on the qualities of inner strength, fearlessness, and confidence in yourself and how you can project them in your world. The spirit of the bear is considered a wise teacher who shows us how to survive in harsh conditions.

Cassie, the bear, an ancient spirit animal worshiped in many traditions is your power animal who is walking with you, especially when you ask for her help to guide you. Since the bear is often associated with shamans in many traditions, this spirit animal can symbolize healing abilities and stepping into the role of the healer. If the bear shows up in your life, it may also be time to take care of your own needs for healing, whether it's at the physical, emotional, or spiritual level. Be sensitive to where you are at and reflect on where you would most need healing. You can call on the bear spirit guidance to direct your energy for meditation, journeying, and art. To help you focus.

The bear is an animal that lives a solitary life. Having a bear as a spirit animal can mean that you find balance and comfort in solitude. The presence of this power animal could point to the need to "regroup" and set up boundaries, so you feel comfortable in your own space. It may be a call to find time away from the crowd or busyness and favor quiet time and rest. You may need to set boundaries or learn to ask for help with your new responsibilities. The bear spirit can also be a great helper to dedicate time and energy to more introspective practices, such as meditation, or art. Call on the spirit of the bear to help you find your center and ground yourself in a strong foundation that will support you in more busy and noisy times. The gift that may assist you on your healing journey.

17. Finding the Original Wound

Carol came into my office holding her solar plexus and obviously in pain. She had received a message from Spirit that she needed a Soul Retrieval, and just learned there was a Shaman in the area. She called for an appointment. After our session, I gave Carol an inspired Message.

My Message to Carol: I am very happy with the results you found on your soul journey, and truly know this is a life changing experience that was meant for you. It is a pleasure working with you and I hope you will return for more Journeying.

The first part of the journey was to find your Wounded self, the part of your soul that split off and shut down your awareness. During the first journeying session, following the sound of the drumbeat, we found deep grief and trauma from events in a past life that showed that in both lives your husband died at a very young age leaving you alone and grief stricken. This caused a veil over your emotions that resulted in living from your shadow self. On the second journey, you discovered that while hunting with your friend, when a deer charged, causing your death, your friend stood by and watched you die without offering to assist you or comfort you. On further questioning, you learned this was the same man who was your husband in previous lives. From that time on, your lives crossed paths and you saw that he was always around you, watching you. On further questioning, you discovered that he had taken an oath, made a soul contract, to always be near you to protect you. Your lives continue to connect even in this lifetime.

Journeying to the Chamber of Healing, you envisioned the white Light filling your body, and every cell and tissue; healing all the grief and pain you were suffering. This pain was affecting your relationships, preventing you from making firm boundaries, and respect for yourself. After shamanic energy healing, the pain was gone, and you began your healing journey.

Before continuing to the Chamber of Grace where you met your healed soul self, we looked at one more life, a happy life where you and the same man were mates. I asked where you were, and you stated, "We are in the Garden of Eden". When asked, were you married, you said, "there was no such thing as marriage then." As the scene opened further you said that you both wore leaves and that you felt complete Joy as you played in the trees.

On your Journey to the Chamber of Grace where you met yourself at age 22, you met a part of your soul that said she contained the Light, and that without the soul light, you are blocked from the Spiritual Light or life force flowing through your body from Source. That this is the Spirit of Life that gives life and immortality. You asked her to integrate with you, returning on the journey together.

On your Journey to the Chamber of Gifts, you found the Goblet. The first meaning could represent that you are filling your vessel with spirit, becoming one with Spirit. Symbolically, the goblet represents that you are now connected to your higher self. When you asked spirit what the goblet is for the reply was, "it is filled with Joy, and where ever you go, you can now spread Joy".

When journeying to find your Animal totem or power animal we descended through the root of the great tree to the very core of Mother Earth where you walked in a beautiful meadow. You sat on a boulder near a lake where the water mirrored everything around you. Setting the intention to find your power animal, you saw a reflection in the water of something behind you, and turning around, saw a white tiger. Making connection with the tiger spirit, you asked if it was your power animal, when it said, "yes", you took its energy into your heart chakra. The White Tiger symbolizes spirit and strength to help you find your personal truth. The White Tiger gives you the ability to trust your intuition and act quickly. It is a great gift when Tiger walks with you.

Journeying to the upper world to meet your Angels or Celestial guides to find your Destiny, you set your intention, asking the question: Who Am I? You were shown an image of a house where two planes crashed into it. Then you were told "You are the Light", like a lighthouse shining light to prevent accidents. Soul journeying changed your life; as you illuminated your shadow and allowed the Light to shine within, you no longer suffered from the trauma that was keeping you in the constant feeling of dread, and whose physical symptoms were pain in your solar plexus. As you embraced the part of you that is light, you became one with Spirit and realized you are the Light, you are enlightened!

Enlightenment may be described as a state of consciousness. The action of having spiritual insight, rebirth, awakened awareness, understanding, and wisdom. You are the Light, integrating your soul with your body, mind, and spirit. This is the journey you are now on; to continue to shine the light of your spirit for others to see. The Light will shine on your path and lead you on your hero's journey spreading light and joy wherever you go. Your last words to me before leaving the session you said, "I'm changed, and the pain is gone".

18. Journey to the Womb of Mother Earth

Shamanism can change the way you perceive your life by opening awareness of how you can rewrite your story, bringing healing and joy instead of pain and suffering. This can begin your Spiritual journey beyond the illusion, opening windows of consciousness into the Heart of the Spiritual realms where you begin to see with eyes of the Heart.

While listening to the Sound of the Drumbeat, the Shaman guides you on a journey deep into your unconscious where everything is stored below consciousness. By setting the intention to discover your memory of the event that caused your wound, you journey down into the womb of Mother Earth, into the root of your understanding. During a time of crisis or of life and death situations, part of the Soul fragments because it cannot dwell in darkness and cannot live in an environment that may be harmful. This part of yourself, your Soul Essence is that part of God's Spirit living in you called your Eternal Soul. Learning the circumstances of your soul loss is the first step towards healing.

On this Journey you will find a memory of the wound that lives in you, and reveals underlying patterns created from the resulting trauma. Energetic cords keep us attached to people with whom we once shared pain or dreams. And just as the maternal cord transports blood to the child, the energetic cords that link us to others are made of emotions and feelings. Just as the Maternal cord is cut at birth, the Shaman cuts energetic cords to allow healthy feelings and emotions to develop.

In the soul retrieval you learn how to illuminate your shadow, so you can reclaim your disowned self as you embark on the inner journey. Remember to trust the process as I guide you, and you listen to the sound of the drum, you are journeying to the realm of magic and intuition, beyond ordinary life.

Prepare for this journey by opening Sacred Space. Sit comfortably as your close your eyes and take your hands into a prayer pose at your heart center. Say the proper intention for this journey, "that you want to see your original wound".

Call on the four cardinal directions: wolf in the south, bear in the west, the ancestors in the north, and the great eagle in the east. Begin breathing to the count of 7, hold, then release. Now follow the sound of the drum as you journey down into the womb of Mother Earth; journey inside the great tree, spiraling down, smell the rich moist soil as you travel down, down, below the surface. Now stand up and look around. You are entering a Sacred Garden in a beautiful green meadow. Envision yourself surrounded by flowers and birds chirping in a nearby forest, make your way to a boulder by a stream and sit for a moment to enjoy the beauty all around you. This is a place you can come to any time for healing and renewal.

Now, I guide my client to imagine a beautiful woman appearing who can nurture them and bring a message. The intention is to heal the first wound, the wound with the Mother. In western culture we have been told we are separate from Mother Earth and that to honor her is a sin against God. This illusion has caused a great divide in our culture and as we can see, women are abused, raped, mistreated, and considered unequal to males. In this patriarchal society women suffer from lack of self- esteem, lack of self-respect, and from the wounds of unworthiness. Just as we live in a society where women are not honored as equal and as "the givers of life", we are also separated from Nature and her energy that supplies support for all life. I find this to be a huge original wound for many women who come to me for treatment of emotional issues stemming from abuse.

During this journey you will be shown the event that separated you from your Soul. That caused Soul fragmentation and the Shadow of illusion that blinds you from seeing your divine birthright. As we call in your guide, you may be led across a stream on a bridge or in a boat. As you follow your guide, you find a pathway leading to a Cave where you go to find your lost soul. You have come here to witness the wound that lives within you, the one that's crucial for your own healing.

Now, as you step into the Cave, you may see many faces of children. Observe; listen, feel, look for a person, call out your name. Open your senses; a sense of touch, a sense of smell and an intuitive sense of what might be going on, you may remember an event that happened when you were a child. The lost soul itself could be a little boy or a little girl. Greet them and ask questions; When did you leave and why did you leave? This child is not the soul part that you're going to retrieve, you'll be bringing back the healed soul when you meet after healing your wound. When you have finished, thank the child for meeting with you, then ask your guide to lead you to the Sacred Garden where can sit on a boulder near a stream, look into the water and reflect on the emotions, on how you feel. Honoring your feelings is the beginning of validating yourself and part of the healing process. The next journey will take you to Healing the Trauma caused by your original wounding.

19. Adam's Story

Adam came to me on a Sunday in great pain. His sciatica was inflamed, and he had difficulty walking. After smudging his aura and opening sacred space, we began the decent into the lower world. Setting the intention of finding his original wound, immediately, he exclaimed, "My Mother's really mad at me!" As the memory unfolded, he said he had been playing outside and fallen out of a tree after a bee stung him. Again, he stated, "My Mother is really mad." In Adam's story, it appears that his mother's anger was his original wound, like a wedge in their relationship.

I began Shamanic Healing using sage, rattles, and energy when he stated, "stuff is coming off my back, there's a huge thorn lodged in my side". I continued vibrational healing and psychic surgery, cutting the energetic cords as I pulled the thorn out. I knew this was causing the pain and inflammation in his Sciatic nerve and that it was a symptom of his repressed emotions caused by the mother wound.

When I interpreted Adam's story, I was shown that his Mother's anger represented a sting, like a bee's stinger that remained in his energy field, growing larger and larger with each passing year. After removing the thorn and healing with light and vibrational energy, healing his emotional body, a new relationship with his mother could began. Later, he told me he had called his mother that night and would continue to work on healing their relationship.

When we journeyed to the Chamber of Grace, Adam was given a new Heart and told that his heart is healing, and he must practice unconditional love for himself and others; then he would receive a gift from spirit to assist him on his journey seeking his destiny. In the chamber of gifts, you received the gift of a keyboard and were told it could be used to write a book or plays addressing bullying in the schools and in ordinary life. Journeying to meet your celestial parents, and to glimpse your destiny, you saw yourself speaking the words of peace to the world. Adam continues the hero's journey to heal himself and give peace and compassion to others.

20. Soul Loss

Following each Soul Retrieval, I am inspired to re-create your story, reflecting the illumination of your healing. Each lifetime we return to continue the work of the inner "collective consciousness", it's a vision that a group or the entire collective hold. The Soul Retrieval assists each person to reunite with spirit, becoming one, to enable you to reach the higher levels of the super consciousness of the soul and begin the hero's journey and fulfilling the dream; the great vision.

Richard came to me out of curiosity; he was walking the Red Road and had participated in the Sun Dance. We began the drumbeat and created sacred space. In the Chamber of Wounds, we saw how a wound has fragmented part of your soul as symbolized by a window closing, then disappearing from you sight; remembering that previously you had taken flight out the window into freedom. You remembered the incident that occurred changed your life, and part of your consciousness was shut. A veil covered your ability to see beyond the illusion of ordinary life because your soul had fragmented.

In the Chamber of Gifts, you received a drum stick that is a symbol of drumming, that is what it is used for; however, it also is symbolic of you drumming out a new rhythm in your life.

In the Chamber of Grace, you saw your soul self; that part of you that is light and is the gift of LIFE itself, your soul essence. In this chamber you saw your archetype as one with the collective unconscious; one with the abilities, hopes, dreams, and visions of the great psychotherapists, such as Carl Jung. There are conditions given for developing integration with your soul; disciplines such as meditation and humbleness. You are being asked to move into soul level healing as a path to your own growth and self-actualization. You must walk the path before you can show others the way. As you pray and ask for the vision to become clearer, you begin to walk the Hero's Journey to your Destiny.

Eagle is your Power Animal, the One who unites you with spirit and gives you wings to fly to higher realms and dimensions. Eagle as archetype, is a messenger between heaven and earth. Because Eagle has great ability to soar high into other realms, into the super conscious realm of the soul, it gives you eyes to see from a higher viewpoint. In time, you may be a messenger of what you are receiving. Flights of the Eagle bring visions, an ability to see into heaven and the collective unconscious; work of the great people of light who are helping the Earth in the Great Plan for Humanity. It's a calling of the soul and may be the work you have been doing in all your lifetimes. Call on (Spirit)Eagle when you are meditating and ask for a vision.

Journey to your Destiny. The journey to your Destiny must be taken by you, it is your life path, your highest destiny. It is like an arrow being shot far into the future and hitting the target; it shows you what is possible because you have seen it. You can see it from a distance, but you must take the journey to get there. While journeying, we saw that you will be a great writer like Jung, or become a Shaman, building bridges between healing modalities. Remember to ask for guidance and allow your Soul to lead the way. Without soul, there is no life; your soul is your Eternal Essence.

21. Soul Contracts

"Your Shadow Self includes emotional and psychological patterns that continue from repressed feelings you do not wish to deal with consciously, or that you are unaware of. Your Shadow also contains the secret reasons why you would sabotage the opportunities that come your way. Confronting Your Shadow requires that you strike out on a healing journey to begin the hero's journey where you have to make choices that exclude the needs of your family or group for your own need to separate yourself".

Caroline Myss, Soul Contracts/Awakening Your Divine Potential

When we begin the Soul Retrieval Journey, it takes us from living from our ego self, living in your shadow, to processing the world of the unconscious where we bring Light to illuminate the truth. Your Shadow is primarily rooted in fears that have been repressed but that continue to direct your behavior and that your conscious mind is not aware of. You continue the behavior rather than face the fact you may be repressing those strong instincts causing dysfunction, and illness. According to Carolyn Myss, "There are seven Shadows that are karmic for energetic ties and Ancestral Soul contracts to release; including abuse, abduction, violence, poverty, illness, abandonment, and betrayal." Soul Retrieval can guide you to find and face your contract and decide to mark it null and void; rewriting the story of your healed Soul Self.

Carolyn Myss says, "deep within our unconscious we feed the energy part of ourselves that maintains our shadow pattern that feeds our soul fragmentation. We may fear our own empowerment because it represents changes in our lives that would remove us from those who love us for being vulnerable, and we fear being empowered because then we can no longer claim we're not responsible for our actions." Soul Contracts, by Caroline Myss

Spiritual initiations occur during Journeying when you face your shadow and view the Soul Contract agreement; often discovering the pattern of dysfunction goes back to an Ancestral wound. During Soul Retrieval, you begin by surrendering to divine guidance. By ending the struggle of your will and divine will, you allow truth to illuminate the Soul Contract made, and with divine assistance declare it "null and void." You then rewrite the contract for your highest possible potential to be realized, and you begin the Journey to healing and discovering the gifts that will assist you to live your divine purpose.

The act of forgiveness frees you to give up the illusion of ordinary life, you cannot make the journey to the upper world without going through your heart. Forgiveness is the key to set yourself free.

In a guided Meditation, while listening to the sound of the Drum, I guide you down into the Root of Mother Earth to find the Soul Contract that you or your Ancestor made. Journeying to your Sacred Garden, you are lead to a nearby stream where you meet your guide who will lead you to find your Soul Contract. The guide takes you to a large room, a huge Library filled with scrolls. One scroll has your name on it. Ask you guide to climb the ladder reaching up to where your scroll is located and return with it. Now, I instruct you to ask your guide to read the Scroll and help you understand its meaning and how it still affects your life. After asking questions, and learning the full meaning of the agreement, thank your guide and return to the Garden where you begin your ascent. My instruction to you is to rewrite the script, the Soul Contract, with the intention of supporting language that describes the life you choose to live and that honors your higher self. Because you have free will, you visualize yourself marking the old agreement "Null and Void" and declare to your unconscious that you are no longer following the old script but now have a new Contract. Give thanks for your healing and open awareness to the new gifts you will receive to assist you on your journey.

All through history we have heard of Soul Contracts made that are binding agreements between two people, or between you and God or you and Evil. Sometimes people have agreed to anything that will serve the purpose of the moment, not realizing the far-reaching results this can have. Ancestors that made binding agreements long ago may affect your life now. Because you have free-will and are on a Journey to be one with the Divine, you have many helpers to support your decision to be free from binding agreements in the past. Ask for guidance and rewrite the story, awaken the Dream and begin to walk in the path of Healing and Light. By setting the intention for future generations to benefit from your new healing, you effect seven generations in the past and seven generation into the future. Healing ripples through your branch of the Tree of Life and is widespread, allowing future generations to follow the path of their Heart and Soul.

22. Angela's Story

Angela stated her intent to journey to find her Ancestral Wound and the Soul Contract agreed to long ago. Immediately, she saw a woman walking frantically up and down the street. Explaining the scene, she began dialogue with the woman whom she recognized as her Aunt. Her Aunt said that she was beside herself, that she had so many children, she was overwhelmed. On further questioning by Angela, her Aunt told her that all the females in her lineage were sworn to an agreement made in the Soul Contract long ago stating that all women were to marry and have lots of children, they were forbidden to work outside the home or have a career.

Angela remembered that all the females in her family were "stay at home Mothers", none had careers or worked outside the home. When we journeyed to view the Soul Contract, after carefully reading the exact words, Angela stamped the contract "null and void", repeating out loud so that the words registered in her subconscious mind. Asking her guide to help her rewrite the best possible contract, Angela agreed in the new agreement that all her female relatives were free to choose the life they wished to live for their highest and greatest good. She was happy with the results, then pictured the old contract burned in the fire. On leaving the session, she said, I feel lighter, freer, and I plan on continuing my career." Angela stepped onto her Journey and new beginning in search of her Destiny.

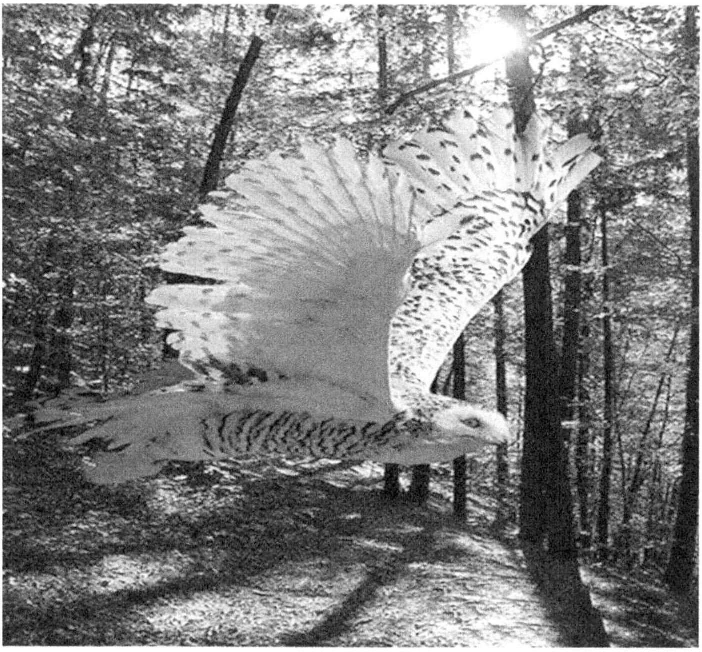

23. Hero's Journey in Search of Your Sacred Destiny

Forgiveness sets you free to evolve your soul as you illuminate your shadow becoming One with the Light. The 7 veils of illusion prevent the Light from filtering into your consciousness, leaving you stumbling in the dark, a victim of fate. Soul retrieval leads you to the Light, for you to embrace and empower yourself by healing the whole you. You are your own best healer, but you must be willing to take the journey into the unknown, to that part of yourself called your shadow. It's very dark there, and unknown, a wilderness. However, if you are willing, you will be equipped with guides to lead and protect you from the darkness all around. It's your journey in search of your soul, your essence, that spark that is eternal.

Denise came to my open house where I explained Soul Retrieval and it's many benefits. She said that she knew she needed help and that "darkness was all around her", she made an appointment. At our first session, I was aware of resistant forces surrounding us and began cleansing with sage and shamanic healing with sound. I called in the 4 protecting Angels to assist with the healing. She commented that she was feeling lighter and wasn't sensing the darkness all around her. During the healing, I focused on pulling off negative energy and asking that it be escorted wherever it should go. We ended the session and she made an appointment for the following week.

I was uncertain that Denise could follow the sound of the drum and my voice. We had cleared the negative energy, and she was willing to continue. We began with a meditation; calling in the supportive angels and animal helpers. Immediately after entering the garden in the lower world, Denise remarked that the Wolf was leading her, and she was feeling more confident to find her original wound. Still frightened of the unknown, Bear came to her side, assuring her that "she had her back" and was walking with her. When we came to the chamber of wounds, she remembered a soul contract, an agreement with the dark that had haunted her and her family lineage all her life. She was shown that the sacrifice she would have to make was to offer forgiveness for the many wrongs she and her family had endured. Eagle lifted her site to a place of great peace and healing as she offered the words that set souls free to evolve and be all they can be.

Eagle rose higher and higher, lifting her awareness to a high peak where she could catch a glimpse of her healed soul self; a Painter; with a sharp sense of the water, its movement, and waves. She was going to paint abstract oil paintings of the Sea. When we ended the session, she was changed. She was now free to go on her hero's journey to become the great Artist she imagined. She said, I'm going to get my easel and paints out of the closet and begin. Later she messaged me, "it worked!"

24. Chamber of Grace

Crystal asked to have a Soul Retrieval after undergoing a complicated operation. She said, "I feel like I'm not here. I'm not in my body". Although she was younger that most clients, I was assured by my spiritual guide that she would benefit from a Healing Session, we already knew that the Trauma of her operation caused her Soul Loss. I had heard of other client's experiences of having difficulty coming back into their body after anesthesiology. They also reported having anxiety; some report how invasive surgery is when a surgical knife opens the Aura. The body lingers without the life force to heal the wound, as energy continues to leak out the hole, and the patient remains weak. The electro-magnetic field around the body called the Aura, must be sealed by an energy healer so that the other causal bodies will heal.

"Grace", by Paul Tillich, "Grace strikes when we are in pain and great despair. It strikes when we feel we have somehow violated another life, a deeper more meaningful life. Like a Wave of Light washing over the darkness, we are made new. We know because we know that we are accepted by One much greater that ourselves. From that time on, we are forever changed."

After creating sacred space, Crystal began Journeying to the rhythm of the Drumbeat. I asked her to set the intention to Journey to the Chamber of Healing and Grace. I began with sage and the rattle to loosen all the energy around her body, smudging to release and remove all trauma and negative energy caused by the illness and subsequent operation. Then using Reiki healing and vibrational energy, I sent Crystal as much energy as she needed. I asked her to imagine herself sitting in the center of the Sun, as I filled the circle around her Aura with Golden Light and sealed it with the Blue Healing Light. Holding the vision of energy filling every cell and every tissue in her body, I visualized her energy body healed. She continued to hold the vision, raising her vibration to a place of well-being.

Journeying to the place of Grace, Crystal set the intention to see her healed Soul Self, her essential self. She immediately said, "I see myself, I'm eighteen years old and I am glowing with Light." I instructed her to ask if her lost soul part was ready to come back with her and she stated, "I'm being told that I have to change my lifestyle, and I have to be less critical of myself. I have to learn to love myself." On further questioning, Crystal's Soul self said that around the age eighteen she would have a spiritual experience, and she would receive the gift of Grace, and her Soul and body would be made whole".

Immediately after the Session, I noticed a change in Crystal's appearance. Before, she had been listless and without an appetite, her color was pale, and she lacked the physical energy to walk and move about. Now, I was seeing rapid improvement before my eyes. She got out of bed and asked to eat a meal. I was pleased that I could help her, confident that her Aura was sealed and now she was healing.

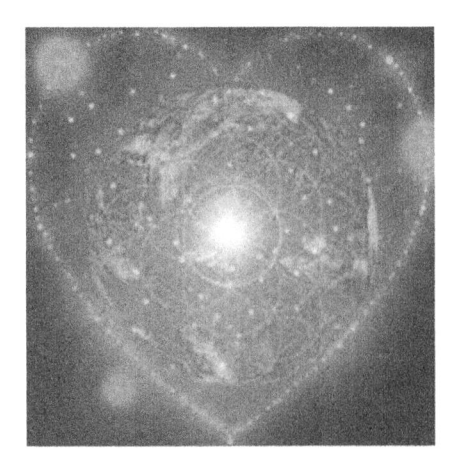

25. Illuminating Your Shadow

After the Soul Journey sessions, I recreate the Story witnessed on each client's journey as part of my Medicine. The following is an example of how my client, Tess, learned to illuminate her shadow and find her destiny. This is the story spirit illuminated for me after her session.

Hi Tess, it was a pleasure doing Soul Retrieval with you, I hope you are reflecting on the good results. I put together a brief story of your journey that may help you interpret your experience and know how powerful it is to become one with your Soul's Light.

After creating sacred space, we began the journey descending into the underworld, following the root of the Great Tree down into the underworld and roots of things. You were met by Squirrel who is one of you animal teachers. Squirrel symbolically comes to remind you to have fun as well as to be prudent in planning for thinner days ahead. Also, there is a higher metaphorical meaning for Squirrel coming into your life. A reminder that "what we sow is what we reap." As Squirrel stores seeds in the earth, she only uses about 10%, the rest is used to seed the earth with new life. Thus, Squirrel is teaching you to also save enough for yourself as well as giving to the Earth.

On your journey to visit your own Sacred Garden, you were accompanied by Squirrel and your guide. This journey was to remind you that you were never separated from the Great Mother, that you are part of the Earth, as well as spirit. It is important to honor yourself and all women. Women are the givers of life, women are the Earth. I hope you will continue to honor yourself and realize that you are a very special daughter. Even as you honor your own Mother, for the woman that she is.

On our Journey to the Chamber of Healing, in this special space, you were filled with the Golden liquid energy of the Sun, healing every cell and tissue, every memory, and blocked emotion. As you were given the symbol of sitting inside the sun, in a Golden Ball of Light, you found your center and brought Light to your wounded self, called your shadow. Trauma and negative energy was pulled off, and your aura sealed with the Light to further your initiation of the Light and Oneness with the Sun and all that is.

The Candelabra is your gift in the Chamber of Treasures. Symbolically this represents the illuminated Tree of Life growing in your body, with the upper branches burning a bright light as the kundalini rises, to continue your spiritual growth. The candelabra is a symbol of bringing light where before there was darkness, illuminating your shadow self. Be sure to light candles as a reminder to continue to bring light to yourself and those around you.

Our journey continued to the Chamber of Grace where you were given the gift of Light and shown your eternal soul that awaits the time when you are ready to receive the gift of life essence, and immortality. This represents a spiritual experience you will have; an initiation of the Light, whereby you will receive immortality while you are living. This includes an awareness that we are all One, that everything is connected in a stream of life. At that time, you are promised a long healthy life.

Our journey to the upper world began as you ascended the spiral stairs to the branch where Eagle was waiting for you. Eagle represents becoming one with spirit. This allows you to journey beyond ordinary life, beyond the illusion, riding the thermals to higher and higher levels of consciousness where you see with eyes of your Heart. Eagle is your constant ally and visionary giving you the ability to fly beyond this realm to the spiritual realms where angels and our celestial parents dwell. You can do this anytime you look into the eye of Eagle, becoming one with Spirit.

Journeying onto the firm surface of the cloud, you called in your Celestial parents who came in the form of White Lights. Lovingly, they read your Soul Contract, reminding you of your purpose for incarnating on Earth. The contract said, "you are to illuminate the Light in yourself and others." This means you have come to Earth to illuminate your shadow, and to remember that you are a Lightworker, spreading healing light to illuminate other's shadows.

I am so honored to share this inspiring message with you. I was such a pleasure to meet you. Continue to shine your light.

26. Becoming Whole

Healing the original wound that causes Trauma is a pathway of healing. The Shaman employs spiritual guidance to help you connect with your spiritual source. You are meant to find rebirth and enlightenment. In Soul Retrieval and Shamanic Healing, you will be gently guided to your recovery into being all that you are meant to be. When you heal, become whole, you experience your highest reality.

Tragedy changes our brain and our everyday functioning. Life altering events create a disconnect with everyone and everything. States of hyper-vigilance and numbness can cycle. Triggers can set off reactivity. Your spiritual life can suffer. Trauma can make you feel detached, irritable, anxious, and highly reactive in numerous ways. It re-wires the brain in an attempt to protect you, but it can actually harm you more.

Traumas highjack our sense of well-being and true purpose. You may have been diagnosed with Post Traumatic Stress Disorder or Acute Stress Disorder. The good news is your brain can recover and be restored. You can live well again or maybe for the first time. Healing the original wound and resulting trauma is a pathway of healing the whole person, reclaiming your full potential and sacred destiny. Trauma doesn't have to leave you stumbling in fate, you can learn to reconnect with yourself and others, as you heal the trauma, illuminating your Soul. You can change the course of your life by focusing on the things that aid your healing. In doing so, the thoughts and reactivity that harm you will diminish over time. You can find your value and purpose and move toward it.

Your healing journey is sacred to you. Your story is unique. You, and only you, know how you feel and more importantly, how you want to feel. Shamanic Healing and Soul Retrieval are practices to bring healing and transformation. Trauma may have infiltrated every part of your life, but you can change what it has done to you. That time was not lost or wasted. It can be viewed with a new perspective.

You will learn that what is operating in your body, mind and spirit is subconsciously holding you to trauma responses. You will be shown how to reconnect with the good life you were born to have, before trauma changed the course of your life. You can heal the past and begin your journey to fulfill your sacred destiny.

The Shaman employs spiritual guidance to help you tap into your powerful healing connection with your spiritual source. You are meant to find rebirth and enlightenment. This body, mind and spiritual guide is an aid to your personal process toward a holistic sense of healing the whole person. In Soul Retrieval you will be gently guided to your recovery into being all that you were created to be. When we heal, become whole, we experience our highest reality.

Drumming creates a sense of connectedness with others that promotes unity and helps raise conscious awareness of the experience of Oneness. As we drum, we raise the resonant field of the collective group that matches the hertz vibrational field of the earth. Drumming circles provide a sense of connectedness with others and interpersonal support. A drum circle provides an opportunity to connect with your own spirit at a deeper level and connect with a group of other like-minded people. Group drumming promotes peace. Drumming unites us with the heartbeat of Mother Earth, raising our vibration as we become ONE Harmonious sound. Rhythm, as a path, leads to the rhythmic roots of all cultures. When we come into the circle and drum, we set the intention for peace, harmony, unity and compassion for all beings. As the vibration rises, we become one united sound, creating a vortex for change. That's why I call it the Universal Language.

Different cultures use the same rhythmic qualities; like the colors of the rainbow, each culture has its own sound and rhythm, yet each is a part of the whole. Although the focus or intent differs from culture to culture, rhythmic drumming has the same power and effects in all traditions. The resonant qualities and attributes of these are universal and come into play whenever we drum. The sound waves produced by the drum impart their energy to the resonating systems of the body, mind, and spirit, making them vibrate in harmony. When we drum, our body, brainwaves, and spiritual energy centers begin to vibrate in response. This resonance leaves reverberating effects up to 72 hours after a drum session. These powerful effects can best be described in terms of their influence on the subtle energy centers known as chakras. There are seven chakras and that the spiritual traditions of the Hopi, Cherokee, and Tibetan and other cultures teach of. There are vibratory centers within the human body referred to as spinning wheels of energy called chakras. There are seven major chakras situated along the vertical spinal axis from the genital region to the crown of the head. Each vortex of energy is associated with a specific color of the rainbow, distinct parts of the body, with particular functions of consciousness. Chakras control the electromagnetic field around the body called the Aura. They are the vitality empowering the physical, mental, and spiritual aspects of one's being. Imbalances in chakras lead to imbalances in body, mind, and spirit. Drumming creates a vibratory resonance that activates, balances, and aligns the chakra system.

The Rainbow Fire symbolizes an illuminated mind and clarity of all aspects of consciousness. It describes the aura of rainbow color light that radiates from a fully activated chakra system. This illumination within allows us to fully integrate the wisdom of all seven centers of consciousness. The fire of clear mind is ever present within each of us, so that each may find the way to unity and harmony. Drumming is one way that we can cultivate the fire of clear mind. The drum's beat ignites the Rainbow Fire within, illuminating the path and showing us the way. With clarity of mind, we can perceive the feeling of Oneness, Unity and Harmony creating a new consciousness. Through the insight and understanding of illuminated mind, we can bring enlightenment to the world!

Native Americans and most of the indigenous peoples of the Earth have known for thousands of years that drumming is a powerful spiritual tool. Only in recent years, though, has the scientific basis come to light. Michael Harner, an anthropologist and founder of the Foundation for Shamanic Studies, did pioneering work in studying the effects of drumming in the 1960s and '70s, outlined in his book, The Way of The Shaman (Harper; San Francisco; 1990). According to Harner, "the beat of the drum, as used to transport native peoples into shamanic states of consciousness, closely approximates the base resonant frequency of the Earth, which can be measured scientifically".

Drumming, by combining the vibrational tones of meditation and the 180-cycles-per-second beat approximating the base resonant frequency of the Earth itself, thus, becomes not only a powerful meditation tool, but a way to tap into our psychic inner ability to travel over vast distances, effect cures, and know, and affect, the future.

Through shamanic journeying, using the drum, we can travel along our energy field lines through those dimensions; in "ordinary," 3-D reality, or the non-ordinary, under world, where we access the unconscious roots, or the upper world, where we access our Divine blueprint and meaning in life. Shamanic, or Native American style drumming is most powerful as a prayerful device; a shamanic journey, using the drum, is visualized prayer. A powerful ancient technology only now being rediscovered by many in the 21st century.

27. See with the Eyes of Your Heart

A Soul Retrieval and the intent of Shamanism is a "Heart Journey"; a spiritual journey to guide you into your heart, and intend to heal you; not only physically, but to promote health- emotional health, stimulate abundance and energy, and awaken your inner intuition. You are A Spiritual Being Having a Physical Experience. Most of the time, most of us lead almost purely physical lives. We need to be able to function and get by in this physical world. However, we are more than just this physical, we are spiritual beings having a physical experience. When we sit still and meditate we can slow our thoughts down and change the focus of our consciousness to get back in touch with our true selves, which can have positive effects on our lives. When we place our attention and consciousness on the heart center then truly amazing results start to happen.

Journeying sessions all have a focus around health and on accessing your heart; helping you leave the physical behind by journeying within your mind to your unconscious and your heart center. They change your point of focus from that which is physically in-front of you, to taking you inside your own body, to your heart. You will create vivid visualizations where you take this mental journey to your heart. As you practice you will see that it becomes more than just imagination, you learn to experience, to feel what it is like to focus your consciousness inside your heart rather than your brain.

You will experience the difference, even in just one or two sessions when you go inside yourself like this and leave the physical world behind even for a short period. You gain a new way of thinking, a new way of looking at the world and at yourself. You also gain a different type of consciousness; a consciousness that comes from your heart, and looks "out" from your heart to examine yourself and the world you live in. You see with the eyes of your Heart. Rather than the "seat" or "home" for your consciousness being your brain or head, it shifts down into your heart. You see the world tinted from an emotional and feeling perspective, rather from a linear and "logical" perspective. Your consciousness comes from love rather than from "logic". The Native Americans refer to this as being in the good mind, or walking the Good Red Road, the Heart Path.

The benefit of using your heart intelligence is the benefit of changing your perspective. Your very consciousness and experience of self in this way; the changes in your life are astounding, from increased energetic and emotional balance, to lower stress and anxiety, and even gaining a powerful sense of intuition which comes from your spiritual self and helps to guide you through life.

Energy and emotional balance are one of the first benefits you will experience in the meditation session itself. This is the sense of balance you feel. During the sessions and as you repeat them you will notice your thoughts slowing down and slipping away, if this is the first time you have tried meditation (successfully) then this might be the first time that you have ever felt real peace without your thoughts racing or your internal voice constantly chatting. However, it is not just during the session that you experience this; it stays with you into your everyday life and with each session it grows and grows. This will help you to gain control of your emotions, and you will be able to keep your energy healthy and positive stopping it from being drained by negative external situations or people in your daily life. This benefit alone will improve your mindset and perspective on life and improves your life in terms of how calm and centered you are, and how happy and positive you are in your day to day life.

Health starts in the mind; your thoughts are the seeds of good (or poor) health. Your mind literally controls the very cells that either age you and cause illnesses or keep you healthy, energetic and youthful. Shamanism puts you in control of your mind as you will focus on sending healing energy out to your physical body and focusing on repairing your body and on improving your health. You will surprise yourself on what is possible when you focus internally at the source of your health and well-being. Take control of your health by taking control of your mind and promoting positive health when you use your heart as your seat of consciousness and send love and positive, healing energy out to your mind and physical body. Shamanism literally helps you rewire your divine blueprint into your life.

When you start to shift your consciousness internally and to experience the world from your heart, rather than purely from your logical brain, you start to open more energetically and emotionally. Your energy is calmer, more balanced, your thoughts aren't racing, you are here in the now and you can think clearly and focus much stronger.

Your heart intuition is activated; literally thinking and feeling from your heart. In this state you will notice the difference in your intuition, in the information you receive, the things you "know" about people and events that come true. You start to find it easier to empathize and connect with people, to share their emotions and to read them. And living like this, developing your heart intuition and using it in your daily life has amazing benefits as you start to perceive people correctly and to make the right decisions; life starts to get a much easier when you heal your shadow and begin to be Soul directed, living from your Heart. Walking in the "good mind" on the Good Red Road.

28. Life is a Ceremony

My Journey in relationship to Mother Earth begins as far back as I can remember when I ran through the fields at about age 6 on my way to the Frog Pond. I remember being aware that the grass was taller than me and all around I could hear the birds and the buzzing sounds of summer. I could feel the wind and see the sea of Oat Fields swaying like waves; and I knew this was my family this is where I belong. I got in touch with the water element at the Frog Pond and went there almost daily because that's where I could look into the water and become calm. The water is an element that reflects our emotions. I learned I could always talk to it and it seemed to reflect back feelings of Peace. Maybe the Ancestors were speaking to me through the water medium. All I know is that when I received enough love and enough energy from the pond I would return home feeling restored.

I always worshipped the Sun, but it was the initiation of the Light that changed my life. One day a Light came down from heaven and entered my head. I was taken up into another realm for many days. I don't know how long I was gone I was only aware that my feet were on the ground and my head was in the clouds. As I look back now that was my first initiation of the Light. The initiation brought a new beginning for me because while I was gone I understood there is no death, and that we do not die, I understood Oneness, we continue as eternal souls connected as One in the ever-evolving whole. The second initiation of Light occurred when a bolt of lightning hit a tree about 4 feet away from where I was standing. I fell down from being within the radius of its power. While on the ground I heard a voice speaking, my heart was beating really fast and I wasn't the same for many days, but I seemed okay. Most of my journey since that time has been to bring the Message of the Light. I continually receive "downloads" from Spirit that I call instructions for living. And I always followed my instructions.

The Medicine Wheel has been an important teacher on my Earth walk. I was born during the Corn Planting Moon in the Month of June. The last stone in the Medicine Wheel before Summer Solstice. Deer is my totem and was the first spirit animal that appeared to me. I was transported in vision outside a dark Forest where Spirit told me to find a path through to the other side. I was instructed to leave my worldview, all my beliefs, by the side of the path. I could take nothing with me. I felt naked and afraid, I was completely in unknown territory. Calling for a guide, White Spirit Deer appeared and guided me on a new pathway through the dark forest and out into a meadow. There I saw the Elders standing in a Circle, and in the middle, the Light was so Bright that I couldn't see their faces. Now I realize, these are the Elders in the Sky World who work closely with our Ceremonies to strengthen the people. After that experience, I was instructed by my inner guidance to move from Colorado to Syracuse. Oh, how I loved Colorado! And the last place I wanted to go was Syracuse, NY. But I began having awake dreams of working with people who were homeless. I knew the Syracuse Rescue Mission was one of the largest homeless shelters in the Country. So that's where I applied for work. I was hired to work as a Medic in the Alcohol Crisis Unit that helped both the homeless street people as well as the alcoholics. Spirit told me that I was learning to expand my heart to love everyone unconditionally and to have no judgment. That I could help people by bringing the Light into the darkness where people could be healed. Syracuse is where I met Chief Shenandoah and learned to walk the Good Red Road.

Deer became my teacher and spirit guide on my path to learning the Great Law of Peace and the Universal Law of One; Chief Shenandoah wore the antlers of authority as his Medicine as Tadodaho, leader and high chief of the Iroquois Confederacy. He became my friend and mentor for many years and continues to guide me from the other side.

The next animal who came to me was a white wolf. She was a husky/wolf my Indian friends gave me for my friendship with the wolf Clan. She taught me loyalty, unconditional love, and how to follow the path. She was my constant companion and in hard Winters when ice formed on the lake and crystals formed on my bedroom wall, water pipes froze, Wolf and I drew close to the fire in the center of the cottage. She was my companion during months of solitary living on the lake and was an important teacher of self-reliance and fortitude.

I learned how to sail when I mastered working with the element Air, the Wind. I am a sailor and at an early age learned that my will and volition create the force needed to draw back the rope putting tension on the Sail creating energy and movement. It seemed I could fly over the water. Sailing was a great lesson that taught me how to read the ripples on the water and to ride the wind thermals. The same lesson taught me how to sharpen my will in what is called volition. It is the tightly focused energy used for reaching a target or desired goal. The object lesson I was shown referred to an arrow and that when you draw back on the bowstring, according to the force of the will and the power of your volition, sends the Arrow as far as possible to hit your target. The target is your possible Destiny. These teachings taught me how to use my Will to create new beginnings and awaken the Dream of how to create future abundance for all generations.

Shaman's Death is an important initiation for becoming a healer or Shaman. There was a time when I was at the end of my life as I knew it, I was in pain and my future looked hopeless. That's when I purposely looked into the darkness and decided to leap, knowing I would die. Yet, in that moment I heard a voice calling and I felt Wings lifting me into the Spiritual world of Light. After this experience my focus shifted as awareness of an invisible world of Spirit became more and more real, and I lived a lifestyle that would allow me to develop lines of communication with the other side. Eagle became my close ally that escorted me back and forth, riding the thermals, seeing with clarity a new point of view that included all the Circle of life. To begin, I created a sacred circle around myself and prepared to receive messages from my spiritual teachers, spirit animals and allies. I was learning to listen to the language of my family in the Invisible world of Spirit.

I have walked the pathway of the Good Red Road, the path of the Heart. By drawing the circle and invoking the four elements. I work within the Sacred Circle that is the space of Creation. The element Fire is an important ally that is a catalyst to experience the Purification of the Heart. I experienced Going Through the Fire of Transformation where I thought I would burn, yet I lived. Fire is the element to burn away the illusion, revealing the Pure Heart of Truth. After an automobile accident that left me injured, my back was like spaghetti and my rotation cups were torn, I surrendered my pain and asked for healing. Spirit told me I had a choice; I could be healed by Spirit, or I could go the way of the world. As soon as I surrendered my brokenness, I felt rays of heat and Light passing over my body all night, it was so hot I thought I would burn. In the morning light I realized I was completely healed from head to toe. I continue to bring the Message of the Light and our ability to Heal ourselves when we are One with Creator, Spirit, and all our helpers in the invisible world.

I continued walking in the Circle of the Medicine Wheel teachings for many years, sharing the teachings in drum circles, and with as many people who were interested. My message was for people to come into the circle and renew their relationship with Mother Earth that was never really broken. It is in the circle where I learned that every living thing is interconnected, both in the physical and invisible worlds. Within this Sacred Space is the vortex for change, the place of creation. Some refer to it as Zero Point or the Void. The Shaman journeys to the space in the Center of the Wheel where there is no time as we know it. In this space of zero gravity, the Shaman travels to all other dimensions by riding the currents into other worlds, seeking communication with the Plant world, the Animal world, or the Mineral world. By creating Sacred Space and moving into the center, the shaman sees into all Dimensions. This is how the Shaman is able to teach people to fly into other spiritual dimensions, how to fly into the Light of the deepest darkest wound and find the Light inside. We do not work alone, but have all our relations that include the elements, angels, animals, plants, minerals, Creator and our personal Spirit guides. We seek to heal by teaching you how to ascend into the Heart of the World where you will see with the eyes of your Heart and understand that we are all One. Then you will know that healing is possible, and peace is possible, because you have free will and can choose to evolve beyond this present darkness, into the Whole where are all One. When we are One we realize our Highest Reality. As Shaman, I have a passion to teach the way of healing and the way of Oneness. It is our birthright to evolve, to ascend in consciousness. The Tree of Life blossoms and Mankind rises. It is the Divine Plan, Heaven and Earth are ONE.

29. The Story of Jumping Mouse

The Story of Jumping Mouse as told by Hyemeyohsts Storm, Seven Arrows, pgs. 68-85.

Once there was a Mouse.

He was a Busy Mouse, Searching Everywhere, Touching his Whiskers to the Grass, and Looking. He was Busy as all Mice are, Busy with Mice things. But, Once in a while he would Hear an odd Sound. He would Lift his Head, Squinting hard to See, his Whiskers Wiggling in the Air, and he would Wonder. One Day he Scurried up to a fellow Mouse and asked him, "Do you Hear a Roaring in your Ears, my Brother?" "No, no," answered the Other Mouse, not Lifting his Busy Nose from the Ground. "I Hear Nothing. I am Busy now. Talk to me Later."

He asked Another Mouse the same Question and the Mouse Looked at him Strangely. "Are you Foolish in your Head? What Sound?" he asked and Slipped into a Hole in a Fallen Cottonwood Tree.

The little Mouse shrugged his Whiskers and Busied himself again, Determined to Forget the Whole Matter. But there was that Roaring again. It was faint, very faint, but it was there! One Day, he Decided to investigate the Sound just a little. Leaving the Other Busy Mice, he Scurried a little Way away and Listened again. There It was! He was Listening hard when suddenly, Someone said Hello.

Hello little Brother," the Voice said, and Mouse almost Jumped right Out of his Skin. He Arched his Back and Tail and was about to Run.

"Hello," again said the Voice. "It is I, Brother Raccoon." And sure enough, It was! "What are you Doing Here all by yourself, little Brother?" asked the Raccoon. The Mouse blushed, and put his Nose almost to the Ground. "I Hear a Roaring in my Ears and I am Investigating it," he answered timidly.

"A Roaring in your Ears?" replied the Raccoon as he Sat Down with him. "What you Hear, little Brother , is the River."

"The River?" Mouse asked curiously. "What is a River?"

"Walk with me and I will Show you the River," Raccoon said.

Little Mouse was terribly Afraid, but he was Determined to Find Out Once and for All about the Roaring. "I can Return to my Work," he thought, "after this thing is Settled, and possibly this thing may Aid me in All my Busy Examining and Collecting. And my Brothers All said it was Nothing. I will Show them. I will Ask Raccoon to Return with me and I will have Proof."

"All right Raccoon, my Brother," said Mouse. "Lead on to the River. I will Walk with you."

Little Mouse Walked with Raccoon. His little Heart was Pounding in his Breast. The Raccoon was Taking him upon Strange Paths and little Mouse Smelled the Scent of many things that had Gone by his Way. Many times he became so Frightened he almost Turned Back. Finally, they Came to the River! It was Huge and Breathtaking, Deep and Clear in Places, and Murky in Others. Little Mouse was unable to See Across it because it was so Great. It Roared, Sang, Cried, and Thundered on its Course. Little Mouse Saw Great and Little Pieces of the World Carried Along on its Surface.

"It is Powerful!" little Mouse said, Fumbling for Words.

It is a Great thing," answered the Raccoon, "But here, let me Introduce you to a Friend."

In a Smoother, Shallower Place was a Lily Pad, Bright and Green. Sitting upon it was a Frog, almost as Green as the Pad it sat on. The Frog's White Belly stood out Clearly.

"Hello, little Brother," said the Frog. "Welcome to the River."

"I must Leave you Now," cut in Raccoon, "but do not Fear, little Brother, for Frog will Care for you Now." And Raccoon Left, looking along the River Bank for Food that he might Wash and Eat.

Little Mouse Approached the Water and Looked into it. He saw a Frightened Mouse Reflected there. "Who are you?" little Mouse asked the Reflection. "Are you not Afraid of being that Far out into the Great River?"

"No, answered the Frog, "I am not Afraid. I have been Given the Gift from Birth to Live both Above and Within the River. When Winter Man Comes and Freezes this Medicine, I cannot be Seen. But all the while Thunderbird Flies, I am here. To Visit me, One must Come when the World is Green. I, my Brother, am the Keeper of the Water."

Amazing!" little Mouse said at last, again Fumbling for Words."

Would you like to have some Medicine Power?" Frog asked."

"Medicine Power? Me?" asked little Mouse. "Yes, yes! If it is Possible."

"Then Crouch as Low as you Can, and then Jump as High as you are Able! You will have your Medicine!" Frog said.

Little Mouse did as he was Instructed. He Crouched as Low as he Could and Jumped. And when he did, his Eyes Saw the Sacred Mountains.

Little Mouse could hardly Believe his Eyes. But there they were! But then he Fell back to Earth, and he Landed in the River!

Little Mouse became Frightened and Scrambled back to the Bank. He was Wet and Frightened nearly to Death.

"You have Tricked me," little Mouse Screamed at the Frog!"

"Wait," said the Frog. "You are not Harmed. Do not let your Fear and Anger Blind you. What did you See?"

"I," Mouse stammered, "I Saw the Sacred Mountains!"

"And you have a New Name!" Frog said. "It is Jumping Mouse."

"Thank you. Thank you," Jumping Mouse said, and Thanked him again. "I want to Return to my People and Tell them of this thing that has Happened to me."

"Go. Go then," Frog said. "Return to your People. It is Easy to Find them. Keep the Sound of the Medicine River to the back of your Head. Go Opposite to the Sound and you will Find your Brother Mice."

Jumping Mouse Returned to the World of the Mice. But he Found Disappointment. No One would Listen to him. And because he was Wet, and had no Way of explaining it because there had been no Rain, many of the other Mice were Afraid of him. They believed he had been Spat from the Mouth of Another Animal that had Tried to Eat him. And they all Knew that if he had not been Food for the One who Wanted him, then he must also be Poison for them.

Jumping Mouse Lived again among his People, but he could not Forget his Vision of the Sacred Mountains.

The Memory Burned in the Mind and Heart of Jumping Mouse, and One Day he Went to the Edge of the Place of Mice and Looked out onto the Prairie. He looked up for Eagles. The Sky was Full of many Spots, each One an Eagle. But he was Determined to Go to the Sacred Mountains. He Gathered All of his Courage and Ran just as Fast as he Could onto the Prairie. His little Heart Pounded with Excitement and Fear.

He Ran until he Came to a stand of Sage. He was Resting and trying to Catch his Breath when he Saw an Old Mouse. The Patch of Sage Old Mouse Lived in was a Haven for Mice. Seeds and many things to be Busy with.

"Hello," said Old Mouse. "Welcome."

Jumping Mouse was Amazed. Such a Place and such a Mouse. "You are Truly a great Mouse." Jumping Mouse said with all the Respect that he could Find. "This is Truly a Wonderful Place. And the Eagles cannot see you here, either," Jumping Mouse said.

"Yes," said Old Mouse," and One can See All the Beings of the Prairie here: the Buffalo, Antelope, Rabbit, and Coyote. One can See them All from here and Know their Names."

"That is Marvelous," Jumping Mouse said. "Can you also See the River and the Great Mountains?"

"Yes and No," Old Mouse Said with Conviction. "I Know the Great River, But I am Afraid that the Great Mountains are only a Myth. Forget your Passion to See Them and Stay here with me. There is Everything you Want here, and it is a Good Place to Be."

"How can he Say such a thing?" Thought Jumping Mouse. "The Medicine of the Sacred Mountains is Nothing One can Forget."

"Thank you very much for the Meal you have Shared with me, Old Mouse, and also for sharing your Great Home," Jumping Mouse said. "But I must Seek the Mountains."

"You are a Foolish Mouse to Leave, there is Danger on the Prairie! Just Look up there!" Old Mouse said, with even more Conviction. "See all those Spots! They are Eagles, and they will Catch you!"

It was hard for Jumping Mouse to Leave, but he Gathered his Determination and Rand hard Again.

The Ground was Rough. But he Arched his Tail and Ran with All his Might. He could Feel the Shadows of the Spots upon his Back as he Ran. All those Spots! Finally he Ran into a Stand of Chokecherries. Jumping Mouse could hardly Believe his Eyes. It was Cool there and very Spacious. There was Water, Cherries, and Seeds to Eat, Grasses to Gather for Nests, Holes to be Explored and many, many Other Busy Things to do. And there were a great many things to Gather.

He was Investigating his New Domain when he Heard very Heavy Breathing. He Quickly Investigated the Sound and Discovered its Source. It was a Great Mound of Hair with Black Horns. It was a Great Buffalo. Jumping Mouse could hardly Believe the Greatness of the Being he Saw Lying there before him. He was so large that Jumping Mouse could have Crawled into One of his Great Horns. "Such a Magnificent Being," Thought Jumping Mouse, and he Crept Closer.

"Hello, my Brother," said the Buffalo. "Thank you for Visiting me."

"Hello Great Being," said Jumping Mouse. "Why are you Lying here?"

"I am Sick and I am Dying" the Buffalo said.

"And my Medicine has Told me that only the Eye of a Mouse can Heal me. But little Brother, there is no such Thing as a Mouse."

Jumping Mouse was Shocked. "One of my Eyes!" he Thought. "One of my Tiny Eyes." He Scurried back into the Stand of Chokecherries. But the breathing came Harder and Slower.

"He will Die." Thought Jumping Mouse. "If I do not Give him my Eye. He is too Great a Being to Let Die."

He Went Back to where the Buffalo Lay and Spoke. "I am a Mouse." he said with a Shaky Voice. "And you, my Brother, are a Great Being. I cannot Let you Die. I have Two Eyes, so you may have One of them."

The minute he Said it, Jumping Mouse's Eye Flew Out of his Head and the Buffalo was Made Whole. The Buffalo jumped to his Feet, Shaking Jumping Mouse's Whole World.

"Thank you, my little Brother," said the Buffalo. "I Know of your Quest for the Sacred Mountains and of your Visit tot he River. You have Given me Life so that I may Give-Away to the People. I will be your Brother Forever. Run under my Belly and I will Take you right to the Foot of the Sacred Mountains, and you need not Fear the Spots. The Eagles cannot See you while you Run under Me. All they will See will be the Back of a Buffalo. I am of the Prairie and I will Fall on you if I Try to Go up the Mountains."

Little Mouse Ran under the Buffalo, Secure and Hidden from the Spots, but with only One Eye it was Frightening. The Buffalo's Great Hooves Shook the Whole World each time he took a Step. finally the Came to a Place and Buffalo Stopped.

"This is Where I must Leave you, little Brother," said the Buffalo.

"Thank you very much," said Jumping Mouse. "But you Know, it was very Frightening Running under you with only One Eye. I was Constantly in Fear of your Great Earth-Shaking Hooves."

"Your Fear was for Nothing," said Buffalo, "For my Way of Walking is the Sun Dance Way, and I Always Know where my Hooves will Fall. I now must Return to the Prairie, my Brother, You can Always Find me there."

Jumping Mouse Immediately Began to Investigate his New Surroundings. There were even more things here than in the Other Places, Busier things, and Abundance of Seeds and Other things Mice Like. In his Investigation of these things, Suddenly he Ran upon a Gray Wolf who was Sitting there doing absolutely Nothing.

"Hello, Brother Wolf," Jumping Mouse said.

The Wolf's Ears Came Alert and his Eyes Shone. "Wolf! Wolf! Yes, that is what I am, I am a Wolf!" But then his mind Dimmed again and it was not long before he Sat Quietly again, completely without Memory as to who he was. Each time Jumping Mouse Reminded him who he was, he became Excited with the News, but soon would Forget again.

"Such a Great Being," thought Jumping Mouse, "but he has no Memory."

Jumping Mouse Went to the Center of his New Place and was Quiet. He Listened for a very long time to the Beating of his Heart. Then Suddenly he Made up his Mind. He Scurried back to where the Wolf Sat and he Spoke.

"Brother Wolf," Jumping Mouse said. ....

"Wolf! Wolf," said the Wolf ....

"Please Brother Wolf," said Jumping Mouse, "Please Listen to me. I Know what will Heal you. It is One of my Eyes. And I Want to Give it to you. You are a Greater Being than I. I am only a Mouse. Please Take it."

When Jumping Mouse Stopped Speaking his Eye Flew out of his Head and the Wolf was made Whole.

Tears Fell down the Cheeks of the Wolf, but his little Brother could not See them, for Now he was Blind.

"You are a Great Brother," said the Wolf, "for Now I have my Memory. But Now you are Blind. I am the Guide into the Sacred Mountains. I will Take you there. There is a Great Medicine Lake there. The most Beautiful Lake in the World. All the World is reflected there. The People, the Lodges of the People, and All the Beings of the Prairies and Skies."

"Please Take me there," Jumping Mouse said. The Wolf Guided him through the Pines to the Medicine Lake. Jumping Mouse Drank the Water from the Lake. The Wolf Described the Beauty to him.

I must Leave you here," said Wolf, "For I must Return so that I may Guide Others, but I will Remain with you as long as you Like."

Thank you, my Brother," said Jumping Mouse. "But although I am Frightened to be Alone, I Know you must Go so that you may Show Others the Way to this Place."

Jumping Mouse Sat there Trembling in Fear. It was no use Running, for he was Blind, but he Knew an Eagle would Find him Here. He Felt a Shadow on his Back and Heard the Sound that Eagles Make. He Braced himself for the Shock. And the Eagle Hit! Jumping Mouse went to Sleep.

Then he Woke Up. The surprise of being Alive was Great, but Now he could See!

Everything was Blurry, but the Colors were beautiful.

"I can See! I can See!" said Jumping Mouse over again and again.

A Blurry Shape Came toward Jumping Mouse. Jumping Mouse Squinted hard but the Shape Remained a Blur.

"Hello, Brother," a Voice said. "Do you Want some Medicine?"

"Some Medicine for me?" asked Jumping Mouse. "Yes! Yes!"

"Then Crouch down as Low as you Can," the Voice said, "and Jump as High as you Can."

Jumping Mouse did as he was Instructed. He Crouched as Low as he Could and Jumped! The Wind Caught him and Carried him Higher."

"Do not be Afraid," the Voice called to him. "Hang on to the Wind and Trust!"

Jumping Mouse did. He Closed his Eyes and Hung on to the Wind and it Carried Higher and Higher. Jumping Mouse Opened his Eyes and they were Clear, and the Higher he Went the Clearer they Became. Jumping Mouse Saw his Old Friend upon a Lily Pad on the Beautiful Medicine Lake. It was the Frog.
"You have a New Name," Called the Frog. "You are Eagle!"

30. Message of the Light

My intention for writing this book and all my programs of teaching; meditation, healing circles, drumming and private healing sessions, is to communicate the Message of the Light among Humanity. To raise the level of human consciousness and so transform the mental and spiritual consciousness of the entire planet to spread the knowledge that there is a Divine Plan for the Ascension of mankind and that this plan has always existed. It is through the creative use of the Mind that men and women can help bring through into outer manifestation the Dream of Oneness. Essentially the human being is a Spirit who came to Earth in the beginning of time to reveal at the End of Time, the cycle of birth, death, and rebirth, that the purpose of man is to evolve beyond mortality and matter with the understanding that our true Essence is eternal and immortal. When we raise our Consciousness and realize we are One with Creator and Mother Earth, with all Creation, we bring Light where before there was Darkness. Our essential understanding must be that we are Light beings come to Earth to manifest heaven on Earth. The essential questions of Life are: who are you and why have you come here? Where did you come from? What is your purpose for being here now? Where are you going? I teach an esoteric teaching of the Light, it's a communication of the Light, and this is a journey of bringing more Light into the interior of the conscious collective, raising your vibrations and Consciousness so that you remember the Divine Truth of your highest reality. I am an Ambassador of Peace on a Mission to communicate the message of the Light among Humanity, to our up rootedness, and separation from universal Oneness, into a unifying power of the Whole. I refer to this as our Journey into the Sun.

We Are presently at the end of the 26000 years cycle of the Earth as we know it. The cycle of birth, death, and rebirth is closing. The cycle of karma has served to help us learn life lessons. Now we are dropping density and descending into the light. What that means is that more light is coming into our density and the vibrations are higher. If we do not clear and drop density along with the Planet, we will not be able to hold the Light as we go through the shift into the next cycle, into the 5th dimension. The Fifth World Native Americans refer to as the world of Peace and Illumination.

Without Light, we will not be able to hold the intense amount of light being poured out as we move through the Shift and resulting Earth changes. The Purpose of this book and all my programs is designed to aid in the process of Soul Evolution and Self-Realization. The call goes forth to heal and become whole by healing mind, body, and spirit. When you integrate your emotional, mental, spiritual, and physical being, you become whole. Healing results when you surrender to the Light, releasing any patterns of behavior that prevent you from realizing and awakening the Dream of your divine Self.

When you realize your highest reality, you are in alignment with God's highest good for your life and for the whole. There is a way, a way into the Silence where you can contact Creator, where you can build communication with the whole of all that is. Now is the time to answer the call.

My Iroquois teachers taught me that nature is the teacher and to learn about the secrets of nature we learn about ourselves. When we go into nature we see in the countless examples surrounding us that all things are evolving because of natural qualities. Everything that we hear, see, sense, touch, intuitively belongs to a powerful Spiritual Essence where all things are an integral whole. The Seneca believe this Spirit or force was in everything and is called the Great Spirit. They believe that Mother Earth is their Mother, by knowing her and her qualities, you discover the role human beings play in the Universal plan. Living in harmony with the peace and quiet of nature teaches us self-discipline. To master this means that we learn how to function harmoniously within our immediate environment.

As we walk in this life journey that is very much an individual Journey, we bring with us natural gifts and talents that are a part of the power that will help us. These gifts and talents could also be called powers and are found in certain truths that are everyone's Birthright. In ancient times the people were initiated into these truths. And the elders taught them how to enter deep within their own inner Consciousness and listen to The Voice waiting to speak. There are ways of learning and understanding that begin at birth and continue until the time of returning to Spirit. As the intensity of Earth changes increase each one of us will feel it in a deep way within ourselves and we will be asked to truly know and understand ourselves and our gifts, and a conscious way so that we may help each other, Mother Earth, and all her children through these difficult times.

As a Shaman, I use Visions and intuition to lead to strong medicine and power that help you create the life that you were born to live. Begin with a Vision Quest, it is a spiritual discipline that allows you to learn wisdom of your body and soul. I learned self-reliance over a long time and that one can rely on their own visions and dreams to provide the direction that illuminates the path they are following. I use Drumming and sound to resonate with the vibration of the Great Spirit. Partnership with the invisible world of spirit trains the Shaman with ability to make personal contact with all the world of the invisible world of spirit and learns how to make personal contact with ancestors and guides, totems and Allies. These personal relationships become our family.

Shamans have an increasing awareness of our responsibility as stewards of all. Shamans develop a total commitment to our beliefs that pervades every aspect of life and enables us to walk in balance with oneself and with our environment. The central focus of our medicine power is this Reliance upon our personal Visions as our guiding force.

It is this Vision that provides the volition and continues to strengthen our will so that we are totally committed to the path. We are a Seeker that must live the commitment every moment. And believe in the unity and Oneness and the evolution of all life-forms as we honor and love all our relations. The Vision Quest is a mystical experience that provides medicine power and is a continued quest for wisdom of our body, mind, and soul. We seek for a single essential force. And the medicine power that ensures personal contact with the invisible World of Spirits to Ascend beyond the world of Illusion which fills the great mystery. We are seeking truth, we have an attitude of acceptance for the unknown and an expanded worldview. We learn to awaken the dream of wholeness and Oneness as we learn to walk on the earth in balance with all life. We have to learn to relate to Creator, to Mother Earth, and each other as well as all creation. All our relations are sacred. The whole Earth is sacred. A Ho.

ABOUT THE AUTHOR

Caroline Dawley is an author, and Administrator of Pathway of Peace Community in Palm Harbor, Florida. She is a Minister, Shaman, Reiki Master, and Healing Practitioner. As a visionary and Shaman, I dedicate my life to working for Creator for the Cause of Peace and Spiritual Healing of the whole person, raising the consciousness of the Planet.

I've been conscious of my spiritual journey for over 40 years after experiencing an awakening to the Light, enlightened; I received deep integrative healing in mind, body, and spirit. I began my inward journey through the heart, healing all issues, and aligning with Creator and the Earth, I began walking a new pathway of wholeness and wellbeing. I hold a Vision of our collective Earth Journey through the Great Central Sun into the New Earth Atmosphere of Oneness and Love. We are born to rise, to evolve, and to learn to fly into the Light of the Darkest Night.

Raven came to me with her black, purple, and shiny translucent colors; she told me she would help me teach people how to fly into the Dark Black Night of their deepest Wound, where they would find their Soul Light, and rekindle their Spirit.

It was then that this Message emerged from Spirit:

"Raven teaches how to fly out of the darkness of the illusion of separation, into the Light where you see we are all interconnected in the Great Mystery. You are a Spiritual Guide teaching people how to fly into the Light of the Dark Night of their Soul by illuminating the Shadow, in the Great Purification of Mother Earth."

Great Spirit can use even the smallest animal to bring a message. This little green lizard appeared on my window screen every day for many days until I listened to her message, "You have a gift that you aren't using that is important for healing the world. Now is the time."

I knew that I had a gift but hesitated to step into it. I was waiting for a sign, to go ahead. Three days later Chief Shenandoah came to me in a dream showing me his Feather Wing used for healing and dusting away evil, the darkness from the most wounded hearts. I looked closely and saw the Thunderbird with all the colors of the rainbow beaded on the wing. And he said, "You now have Thunderbird Medicine".

Made in the USA
Columbia, SC
08 August 2018